delicious
low-carb
desserts

Karin Cadwell, Ph.D., R.N.

STERLING PUBLISHING CO., INC.

NEW YORK

Library of Congress Cataloging-in-Publication Data

Cadwell, Karin.
  Delicious low-carb desserts / Karin Cadwell.
    p. cm.
  Includes index.
  ISBN 1-4027-2349-0
  1. Low-carbohydrate diet—Recipes. 2. Desserts. I. Title.

RM237.73.C33 2005
641.5'6383—dc22

2005012576

10 9 8 7 6 5 4 3 2 1

Published by Sterling Publishing Co., Inc.
387 Park Avenue South, New York, NY 10016
© 2005 by Karin Cadwell
Distributed in Canada by Sterling Publishing
c/o Canadian Manda Group, 165 Dufferin Street
Toronto, Ontario, Canada M6K 3H6
Distributed in Great Britain by Chrysalis Books Group PLC
The Chrysalis Building, Bramley Road, London W10 6SP, England
Distributed in Australia by Capricorn Link (Australia) Pty. Ltd.
P.O. Box 704, Windsor, NSW 2756, Australia

Sterling ISBN 1-4027-2349-0

For information about custom editions, special sales, premium and
corporate purchases, please contact Sterling Special Sales
Department at 800-805-5489 or specialsales@sterlingpub.com.

recipe list

cakes and cupcakes 15

toppings and glazes 27

cheesecakes, tarts, and flans 33

cookies and squares 41

Swedish Gingersnaps
Dream Cookies
Thumbprint Cookies
Almond Rusks
Sweet Potato Cookies
Piña Colada Squares
Walnut Spice Kisses
Rice Krispies-and-Date Squares
Apple Squares
Café au Lait Squares
Langues-de-Chat
Cream Cheese Cookies

pies and tortes 59

Pumpkin-Apple Pie
Lemon Meringue Torte
Blueberry-Yogurt Pie
Double Blueberry Pie
Apricot Cream Pie
Lime Chiffon Pie
Lemon Chiffon Pie
Raspberry Shimmer Pie
Raspberry Ribbon Pie
Raspberry Cream Pie
Hawaiian Pineapple Pie
Peach Cream Cheese Pie
Strawberry Ice Cream Pie
Banana Cream and Strawberry Pie
Strawberry Cream Cheese Pie
Strawberry Meringue Pie
Pumpkin Ice Cream Pie
Butterscotch Pie
Chocolate Chocolate Pie
Coffee and Cream Pie
Blueberry–Sour Cream Pie
Quick Custard Pie
Sour Cream Pie
Cocoa Chiffon Pie

fruit

puddings, custards, and gelatins

meringues 153

cream puffs 175

introduction

I was intrigued by Dr. Robert Atkins's ideas about carbohydrate controlled dieting after reading through his writings on the subject more than twenty-five years ago, and felt compelled to try the diet myself. Unlike the calorie limiting diets I had previously followed, with poor results, cutting down on carbs really worked for me. I lost weight and felt great!

Atkins attributed his ideas to William Banting, whose "Letter on Corpulence, Addressed to the Public," published in London in 1863, proclaimed that a lowered carbohydrate diet resulted in weight loss without hunger. Current research has confirmed Banting's original observation and low-carb dieting has found contemporary support.

Many of us who have tried low-carb dieting would agree with Banting that this way of eating doesn't have to mean feeling hungry all the time. We have found that carbohydrate-laden foods actually make us even more hungry. High-carb diets are associated with an increased risk of health problems such as obesity and type 2 diabetes.

The United States Surgeon General issued the following statement about obesity on May 27, 2004: *The primary concern of overweight and obesity is one of health and not appearance.*

The Surgeon General listed the following consequences of obesity:

Premature Death
- An estimated 300,000 deaths per year may be attributable to obesity.
- The risk of death rises with increasing weight.
- Even moderate weight excess (10 to 20 pounds for a person of average height) increases the risk of death, particularly among adults aged 30 to 64 years.

- Individuals who are obese (BMI > 30) have a 50% to 100% increased risk of premature death from all causes over individuals with a healthy weight.

Heart Disease
- The incidence of heart disease (heart attack, congestive heart failure, sudden cardiac death, angina or chest pain, and abnormal heart rhythm) is increased in persons who are overweight or obese (BMI > 25).
- High blood pressure is twice as common in adults who are obese than in those who are at a healthy weight.
- Obesity is associated with elevated triglycerides (blood fat) and decreased HDL cholesterol ("good cholesterol").

Diabetes
- A weight gain of 11 to 18 pounds increases a person's risk of developing type 2 to twice that of individuals who have not gained weight.
- Over 80% of people with diabetes are overweight or obese.

Cancer
- Overweight and obesity are associated with an increased risk for some types of cancer, including endometrial (cancer of the lining of the uterus), colon, gall bladder, prostate, kidney, and postmenopausal breast cancer.
- Women gaining more than 20 pounds from age 18 to midlife double their risk of postmenopausal breast cancer, compared to women whose weight remains stable.

Breathing Problems
- Sleep apnea (interrupted breathing while sleeping) is more common in obese persons.
- Obesity is associated with a higher prevalence of asthma.

Arthritis
- For every 2-pound increase in weight, the risk of developing arthritis is increased by 9% to 13%.
- Symptoms of arthritis can improve with weight loss.

Reproductive Complications
- Complications During Pregnancy
- Obesity during pregnancy is associated with increased risk of death in both the baby and the mother and increases the risk of maternal high blood pressure by 10 times.

- In addition to many other complications, women who are obese during pregnancy are more likely to have gestational diabetes and problems with labor and delivery.
- Infants born to women who are obese during pregnancy are more likely to have high birthweight and, therefore, may face a higher rate of Cesarean section delivery and low blood sugar (which can be associated with brain damage and seizures).
- Obesity during pregnancy is associated with an increased risk of birth defects, particularly neural tube defects, such as spina bifida.
- Obesity in premenopausal women is associated with irregular menstrual cycles and infertility.

Additional Health Consequences
- Overweight and obesity are associated with increased risks of gall bladder disease, incontinence, increased surgical risk, and depression.
- Obesity can affect the quality of life through limited mobility and decreased physical endurance as well as through social, academic, and job discrimination.

Children and Adolescents
- Risk factors for heart disease, such as high cholesterol and high blood pressure, occur with increased frequency in overweight children and adolescents compared to those with healthy weight.
- Type 2 diabetes, previously considered an adult disease, has increased dramatically in children and adolescents. Overweight and obesity are closely linked to type 2 diabetes.
- Overweight adolescents have a 70% chance of becoming overweight or obese adults. This increases to 80% if one or more parent is overweight or obese.
- The most immediate consequence of overweight, as perceived by children themselves, is social discrimination.

Benefits of Weight Loss
- Weight loss, as modest as 5% to 15% of total body weight in a person who is overweight or obese, reduces the risk factors for some diseases, particularly heart disease.
- Weight loss can result in lower blood pressure, lower blood sugar, and improved cholesterol levels.

- A person with a Body Mass Index (BMI) above the healthy weight range may benefit from weight loss, especially if he or she has other health risk factors, such as high blood pressure, high cholesterol, smoking, diabetes, a sedentary lifestyle, and a personal and/or family history of heart disease.

The results of several recent well-designed clinical trials have indicated that low-carb diets are as good as, and maybe even better than, lowfat diets in helping very overweight people shed pounds quickly. And study participants in the low-carb groups found it easier to stick to their diet than people who were assigned to the low-fat diets. In addition, the study participants in the low-carb diet groups reported decreased LDL ("bad cholesterol") and increased HDL ("good cholesterol"). The low-carb dieters also reported decreased triglycerides, the components of blood that carry fat and are associated with increased risk of heart disease. This is all great news for people who want to adopt a way of eating that's lower in carbohydrates.

Many of my friends have complained to me that they would really like to cut back on carbs and lose weight for health reasons, but they find it hard to give up sweet treats and desserts. Others have complained to me that store-bought low-carb cookies, candies, and desserts give them GI upsets and problems because of the commercial sugar substitutes used in these products. This book is written for people who want to follow a low-carb diet but love yummy sweet treats and desserts.

Shopping and Preparation Hints

Some of the recipes in this book call for sugar, some for sugar substitutes. All are low in carbs, even the ones that use sugar! When I call for sugar substitutes (usually by the packet), I've left the choice of which one to use to you. Choose from saccharine, Nutrasweet®, ace-K®, or Splenda®—whichever you like best. The packs are all about the same in sweetening power but taste different to different people. For a few recipes you will need the kind of sugar substitute that comes in bulk packaging referred to as measures-like-sugar.

I like to use frozen low-fat non-dairy whipped topping (such as COOL WHIP®) and call for it in many recipes. It's low in both carbs and fat and works great as a garnish.

In some recipes I call for either butter or margarine. They have the same number of calories and neither has carbs. If you choose to use margarine, it must be stick margarine, not the easy spreading tub kind, for the recipe to work properly. I have also called for "fat-free butter and oil replacement" in some recipes. I like this product for baked goods. You can find it in the baking supplies section of your supermarket. Where this is called for you can use butter or margarine if you prefer.

Some recipes call for a prepared pie crust. You can use any kind of pie crust you like, either baked from scratch from your favorite recipe or a frozen prepared pie crust from the supermarket.

Best Wishes and Good Health.

Karin Cadwell

thank you to all my marvelously supportive family and friends. Thank you especially to Kajsa, Chuck, Anna, and Elyse.

cakes
and cupcakes

cupcakes
with a cherry on top

These cupcakes are delicious with Cream Cheese Icing (page 28).

- 1 cup all-purpose flour
- 1 package (4 servings) sugar-free vanilla pudding mix (not instant)
- 1¼ cups water or skim milk
- 1½ teaspoons baking powder
- 3 tablespoons fat-free butter and oil replacement product, or margarine, butter or oil
- 2 large eggs or equivalent egg substitute
- 1 teaspoooon vanilla extract
- ½ cup skim milk
- 16 whole maraschino cherries
- 1 recipe Cream Cheese Icing (page 28)

Preheat the oven to 350°F and line two 8-hole muffin tins with baking cups.

Combine the flour, pudding mix, water, and baking powder in a large bowl. Beat in the butter replacement, eggs, and vanilla. Beat for 1 minute, then beat in the ½ cup milk. Fill the muffin tins two-thirds full.

Bake for 15 to 17 minutes, or until a tester inserted in a cupcake comes out clean. Let cool for a few minutes before removing from the tin, then let cool completely on a wire rack. Frost the muffins and top each one with a maraschino cherry.

YIELD: *16 cupcakes* EACH CUPCAKE CONTAINS: *Carbohydrates:* 14 grams *Calories:* 72

hot milk sponge cake

This is one of my grandmother's recipes, which I've updated to include sugar substitute. The hot milk takes the place of some of the eggs that are used in traditional sponge cake.

1 cup cake flour, sifted
1 teaspoon baking powder
3 large eggs
¼ cup granulated sugar
3 packets sugar substitute
¼ cup hot milk
1 teaspoon vanilla extract
1 cup fresh or frozen and defrosted unsweetened berries
1 cup frozen lowfat non-dairy whipped topping, thawed

Preheat the oven to 350°F. Grease two 8-inch round cake pans.

Combine the flour and baking powder in a medium bowl. Lightly dust the cake pans with some of the flour mixture. Using an electric mixer at high speed, beat the eggs in a small, deep bowl until they are light and fluffy, then slowly beat in the sugar and sugar substitute until the mixture is almost double in volume and very thick. Reduce the speed to low, then beat in the hot milk and vanilla. Fold in the flour mixture, a third at a time, until just blended. Pour into the prepared pans.

Bake for 15 to 20 minutes, or until the centers spring back when lightly pressed with a fingertip. Place the pans on wire racks to cool for 10 minutes, then loosen the cakes carefully around the edges with a butter knife and turn out onto the wire racks to cool completely. Let cool right side up on the rack.

Before serving, drain the berries if they have been frozen. Mix the berries with topping. Place between layers and as a garnish on top of the cake.

YIELD: *8 servings* EACH SERVING CONTAINS: *Carbohydrates:* 15 grams *Calories:* 108

chocolate éclair cake

I made this simple, impressive looking, and delicious tasting cake for my mother's 75th-birthday party, to rave reviews.

DOUGH

1 cup water

½ cup canola oil

1 cup all-purpose flour

4 large eggs

1 teaspoon butter-flavored extract

FILLING

2 (8-ounce) packages (4 servings each) sugar-free vanilla instant
    pudding mix

2½ cups skim milk

¾ cup frozen lowfat non-dairy whipped topping, thawed

TOPPING

6 tablespoons unsweetened cocoa powder

2 tablespoons canola oil

2 tablespoons skim milk, plus more if needed

¾ cup sugar substitute

1 teaspoon vanilla extract

1 teaspoon butter-flavored extract

To make the dough, preheat the oven to 400°F. Place the water and oil in a large saucepan over high heat and bring to a rolling boil. Reduce the heat to low and stir in the flour until the mixture forms a ball. Remove from the heat. Using a handheld electric mixer, beat in the eggs thoroughly one at a time. Add the butter-flavored extract. Spoon the dough in the shape of a ring or wreath onto an ungreased cookie sheet.

Bake for 35 to 40 minutes, or until golden brown and dry. Cool in a draft-free spot.

Meanwhile, make the filling. Whisk the pudding mix and milk together in a large bowl until the mixture thickens. Fold in the whipped topping.

To make the topping, place the cocoa powder, oil, and milk in a medium saucepan over medium heat and stir to dissolve the cocoa powder. Remove from the heat and cool. Add the sugar substitute, vanilla, and butter-flavored extract and beat until glossy and smooth. Add a little extra milk if necessary, one teaspoon at a time.

To assemble, cut the cake in half horizontally and place it on a serving plate. Remove the top half, spread the filling over the bottom, and replace the top. Drizzle the topping over the cake.

YIELD: *24 servings* EACH SERVING CONTAINS: *Carbohydrates:* 15 grams *Calories:* 100

irish jam cake

All-fruit jams and jellies usually need to be diluted with a little water to make them spreadable. Fresh berries are a lovely garnish for this light and lovely cake.

1¾ cups cake flour
¾ teaspoon baking powder
⅛ teaspoon salt
4 large eggs or equivalent egg substitute, at room temperature
½ cup granulated sugar
1 teaspoon grated lemon rind
¾ teaspoon lemon extract
½ cup all-fruit blueberry jam

Preheat the oven to 350°F. Grease and flour two 8-inch round cake pans and line the bottom of each with parchment or wax paper. Sift together the flour, baking powder, and salt into a small bowl and set aside. Using an electric mixer at high speed, beat the eggs until they are thick and lemon colored. Gradually beat in the sugar. Using a spatula, fold in the flour mixture, lemon rind, and lemon extract.

Pour the batter into the cake pans and bake for 20 to 25 minutes, or until a toothpick inserted in the center comes out clean. Cool slightly in the pans before turning out onto a cooling rack. Remove the parchment immediately. Let cool right side up on the racks. Cool completely, then place one layer on a serving plate. Stir in a small amount of water to the jam to make it a spreadable consistency. Spread the jam over the first layer and place the second layer on top.

YIELD: *12 servings* EACH SERVINGS CONTAINS: *Carbohydrates:* 29 grams *Calories:* 164

devil's food mayonnaise cake

With fat-free mayonnaise to cut down on the calories, you'd never guess this wasn't authentic devil's food.

1 cup cold water
2 teaspoons baking soda
1 cup fat-free mayonnaise
¼ cup unsweetened cocoa powder
¼ cup granulated sugar
¼ cup measures-like-sugar sugar substitute
2 cups all-purpose flour
1 teaspoon vanilla extract
2 cups frozen lowfat non-dairy whipped topping, thawed

Preheat the oven to 350°F. Grease and flour two 8-inch round cake pans.

Pour the water into a large mixing bowl and add the baking soda. Stir to dissolve the baking soda, then stir in the mayonnaise, cocoa powder, sugar, and sugar substitute. Add the flour, baking soda mixture, and vanilla and beat until smooth.

Pour the batter into the prepared pans and bake for 30 to 35 minutes, or until cake tester inserted into middle of cake comes out clean. Cool slightly in the pan before removing to a rack to cool completely. Let cool right side up on the rack. Top with the whipped topping to serve.

YIELD: *10 servings* EACH SERVING CONTAINS: *Carbohydrates:* 22 grams *Calories:* 132

tomato soup cake

This is a low-carb version of a Depression-era recipe, popular then because eggs were so expensive. It tastes even better after it's been refrigerated for awhile.

¼ cup granulated sugar

½ cup canola oil

2 cups all-purpose flour

1 teaspoon ground cinnamon

1 teaspoon ground nutmeg

1 teaspoon ground cloves

1 teaspoon baking soda

1 teaspoon baking powder

¼ cup measures-like-sugar sugar substitute

1 (10-ounce) can tomato soup

1 cup raisins

CREAM CHEESE FROSTING

1 (3-ounce) package fat-free cream cheese

1 cup measures-like-sugar sugar substitute

1 teaspoon vanilla extract

1 tablespoon evaporated skim milk

1 teaspoon butter-flavored extract

Preheat the oven to 350°F. Coat a loaf pan with nonstick cooking spray.

Combine the sugar and oil in large bowl. Sift the dry ingredients together into a separate large bowl and add them to the sugar-oil mixture. Mix well. Add the soup and raisins.

Turn the batter into the prepared loaf pan and bake for 45 minutes, or until cake tester inserted in middle of cake comes out clean. Cool slightly in the pan before removing to a wire rack to cool completely.

Meanwhile, to make the frosting, using an electric mixer at high speed, whip all the frosting ingredients together until mixture is smooth. Frost the cake just before serving.

YIELD: *24 servings* EACH SERVING CONTAINS: *Carbohydrates:* 15 grams *Calories:* 143

strawberry layer cake

This unusual recipe is adapted from a traditional Swedish recipe. My family enjoys it to top off a simple dinner. It's best served within six hours of making.

3 large eggs or equivalent egg substitute
¼ cup granulated sugar
3 packets sugar substitute
1 cup all-purpose flour
2 teaspoons baking powder
½ cup margarine or unsalted butter, melted
1 cup unsweetened applesauce
10 ounces frozen unsweetened strawberries, thawed
Frozen lowfat non-dairy whipped topping, thawed, for serving

Lightly oil a 6- to 8-inch skillet or griddle and place over low heat. Using an electric mixer at high speed, beat the eggs, sugar, and sugar substitute together until thick. Sift together the flour and baking powder into a medium bowl. Add the flour mixture to the egg mixture and mix gently by hand. Add the margarine and mix gently. Pour one-third of the batter into the skillet. Cook as pancakes, turning only after bubbles have appeared. Turn onto a plate. Repeat twice, to make 3 layers. Blend the applesauce and strawberries together in a medium bowl. Spread a layer of fruit between each of the 3 layers and on top. Top with your favorite whipped topping.

YIELD: *8 servings* EACH SERVING CONTAINS: *Carbohydrates:* 15 grams *Calories:* 162

french pastry cake

One word for this cake—"wow!" It's an impressive dessert to serve at a dinner party but easy enough to make for an everyday meal. It would have been out of this world in fat and calories before the new fat-free ingredients entered the scene, but no one will know that you've used them here.

½ cup margarine or unsalted butter
½ cup fat-free cream cheese
¼ cup granulated sugar
½ cup measures-like-sugar sugar substitute
2 large eggs or equivalent egg substitute
1 cup fat-free sour cream
1 cup fat-free mayonnaise
1 tablespoon vanilla extract
2 cups all-purpose flour
1 teaspoon baking powder
1 teaspoon baking soda

CINNAMON TOPPING
1 tablespoon ground cinnamon
2 packets sugar substitute
½ cup chopped almonds

Preheat the oven to 350°F. Coat a tube pan or Bundt pan with nonstick cooking spray.

Cream the margarine and cream cheese with the sugar and sugar substitute in a large bowl. Add the eggs, sour cream, mayonnaise, and vanilla and beat well. Combine the flour, baking powder, and baking soda in another bowl and fold into the batter.

To make the cinnamon topping, mix together the cinnamon, sugar substitute, and chopped almonds in a small bowl. Pour half the batter into the pan. Sprinkle half the cinnamon topping over the batter. Add the rest of the batter and top with the remaining cinnamon topping.

Bake for 60 to 75 minutes, or until the top is lightly browned and the cake pulls away from the pan.

YIELD: *20 servings* EACH SERVING CONTAINS: *Carbohydrates:* 15 grams *Calories:* 155

snowball cake

Impressive! Prepare this cake any time you want to show off—it looks fabulous on a buffet table.

1 package (4 servings) sugar-free strawberry gelatin mix
1 cup hot water
1 cup cold water
1 cup frozen lowfat non-dairy whipped topping, thawed
2 cups fresh or frozen and thawed unsweetened strawberries
1 angel food cake, cut into 1-inch cubes

Prepare the gelatin by placing the powder into a large bowl. Add the hot water and stir until the powder is dissolved. Add the cold water and stir to combine. Refrigerate about an hour, until partially set. In another bowl, fold together the whipped topping and the strawberries. Fold into the partially set gelatin and return to the refrigerator.

Line a deep bowl with long pieces of wax paper. The pieces should extend from over the edge, travel down the inside of the bowl, and go up the other side, extending past the rims. Use several overlapping strips so the inside of the bowl is totally covered. Fill the bowl with alternate layers of the gelatin mixture and the cake cubes.

Refrigerate at least 8 hours or overnight. To remove, place a cake plate upside down on top of the bowl. Turn the whole thing over and carefully peel off the wax paper.

YIELD: *16 servings* EACH SERVING CONTAINS: *Carbohydrates:* 25 grams *Calories:* 112

orange-walnut cupcakes

Be careful to measure out the flour lightly, so you have just the right amount, otherwise these cupcakes will become too heavy.

- 2 cups all-purpose flour
- 2 tablespoons granulated sugar
- 1 tablespoon baking powder
- 1 cup water
- 2 teaspoons grated orange peel
- 1 teaspoon orange extract
- ½ teaspoon butter-flavored extract
- 2 large egg whites
- ¼ cup finely chopped walnuts
- 1 tablespoon brown sugar

Preheat the oven to 400°F. Coat a 12-hole muffin tin with nonstick cooking spray.

In a large bowl, whisk together the flour, granulated sugar, and baking powder. In another bowl, mix together the water, orange peel, orange extract, butter-flavored extract, and egg whites. Pour the wet mixture over the dry mixture and stir lightly to moisten. Do not beat or over-stir. In a third bowl, combine the walnuts and brown sugar.

Spoon the batter into the muffin tins and top with the nut mixture. Bake for 14 to 16 minutes, or until a toothpick inserted in the middle of a muffin comes out clean. Cool for a few minutes before removing from the tin, then cool completely on a wire rack before serving.

YIELD: *12 cupcakes* EACH CUPCAKE CONTAINS: *Carbohydrates:* 20 grams *Calories:* 107

toppings and glazes

cream cheese icing

S imply decadent!

   ¼ cup unsalted butter or margarine
   8 ounces fat-free cream cheese
   3 packages sugar substitute
   2 teaspoons vanilla extract

Beat together all the ingredients in a medium bowl until smoothly blended.

YIELD: *¾ cup* EACH TABLESPOON CONTAINS: *Carbohydrates:* 1 gram *Calories:* 5

strawberry topping

S erve this over low-carb ice cream, angel food cake, sponge cake, crêpes, or even cream puffs.

   2 (16-ounce) packages frozen unsweetened, sliced strawberries, thawed
   5 teaspoons cornstarch
   ½ cup all-fruit strawberry jam

Drain one package of the frozen strawberries and set aside. Place the other package of strawberries, the cornstarch, and jam in a blender or food processor and mix until well blended. Pour the mixture into a small saucepan and cook over medium heat, stirring constantly, until thickened and bright, about 3 to 5 minutes. Remove from heat and add the drained strawberries. Serve warm or cold. The topping will keep in the refrigerator for a week.

YIELD: *4 cups* 1 TABLESPOON CONTAINS: *Carbohydrates:* 4 grams *Calories:* 24

not-too-sweet
chocolate sauce

This chocolate sauce stores well refrigerated; just warm gently before serving. It's great over low-carb pudding or frozen treats.

3 tablespoons unsweetened cocoa powder
1 tablespoon all-purpose flour
1½ cups skim milk
2 tablespoons unsalted butter or margarine
1 tablespoon sugar substitute
1 teaspoon vanilla extract
½ teaspoon butter-flavored extract

Combine the cocoa powder and flour in the top of a double boiler placed over simmering water. Add the milk and stir until free of lumps. Cook, stirring, until thick and smooth, about 5 minutes. Remove from heat and stir in the butter. Cool for 15 minutes, then stir in the sugar substitute, vanilla, and butter-flavored extract.

YIELD: *24 servings*   EACH TABLESPOON CONTAINS: *Carbohydrates:* 2 grams *Calories:* 18

raspberry sauce

S eedless raspberry preserves work best in this recipe and are worth hunting down.

½ cup all-fruit seedless raspberry preserves
2 tablespoons Chambord or raspberry brandy
2 tablespoons water

Place the preserves into a small saucepan. Add the Chambord and water. Mix well with a wire whisk. Place over medium heat and heat gently, stirring constantly, until well combined.

YIELD: *12 tablespoons*   EACH TABLESPOON CONTAINS: *Carbohydrates:* trace *Calories:* 4

chocolate glaze

Y ou can add extra milk to get the right consistency if the glaze is too thick. The sauce is great drizzled over cream puffs or sponge cake.

2 tablespoons unsweetened cocoa powder
2 tablespoons skim milk
2 tablespoons fat-free cream cheese
2 teaspoons sugar substitute

Place the cocoa powder and milk in a small bowl and stir to moisten the cocoa. Using a fork, beat in the cream cheese until smooth. Add the sugar substitute and mix well.

YIELD: *7 tablespoons*   EACH TABLESPOON CONTAINS: *Carbohydrates:* 2 grams *Calories:* 10

napoleon fudge topping

R ich and creamy, this topping rivals that which you'll find in the finest bakeries.

- **2 tablespoons unsweetened cocoa powder**
- **1 teaspoon canola oil**
- **2 teaspoons skim milk**
- **2 teaspoons sugar substitute**
- **½ teaspoon vanilla extract**
- **⅛ teaspoon butter-flavored extract**

Place the cocoa powder in a small saucepan. Add the oil and milk and whisk to combine. Heat gently over low heat, stirring constantly, until the mixture is well blended and heated. Remove from the heat. Stir in the sugar substitue, vanilla, and butter-flavored extracts and mix well. Serve warm.

YIELD: *enough for 2 toppings*   EACH TABLESPOON CONTAINS: *Carbohydrates:* 4 grams *Calories:* 48

mocha glaze

D rizzle this glaze over crêpes, cream puffs, or low-carb ice cream for a coffee-chocolate accent.

2 tablespoons unsweetened cocoa powder

2 teaspoons instant coffee powder

2 tablespoons hot water (more if needed to get the consistency you want)

2 tablespoons fat-free cream cheese

2 teaspoons sugar substitute

Combine the cocoa powder and instant coffee powder in a medium bowl. Add the hot water and stir until the mixture is smooth and evenly moist. Beat in the cream cheese and sugar substitute until smooth.

YIELD: *10 tablespoons* EACH TABLESPOON CONTAINS: *Carbohydrates:* 1 gram *Calories:* 5

cheesecakes,
tarts, and flans

low-carb cheesecake

This is a low-carb version of the old-fashioned cheesecake everyone loves. You'll need to make the yogurt cheese a day ahead.

¼ cup graham cracker crumbs
2 cups yogurt cheese (see Note)
2 teaspoons vanilla extract
½ cup egg substitute
2 tablespoons cornstarch
6 packets sugar substitute

TOPPING
½ cup fat-free sour cream
2 teaspoons granulated sugar
2 teaspoons sugar substitute
1 teaspoon vanilla extract

Preheat the oven to 325°F. Spray a 9-inch springform or other pie pan with non-stick cooking spray. Sprinkle it evenly with graham cracker crumbs and set aside.

Using a handheld electric mixer at medium speed, beat the yogurt cheese, vanilla, egg substitute, cornstarch, and sugar substitute together in a large bowl until creamy. Pour the mixture into the pan over the crumbs.

Bake for 35 minutes. Remove from the oven and place on a rack to cool, then refrigerate until cold. When ready to serve, preheat the oven again to 325°F. Combine the topping ingredients in a small bowl and pour the mixture over the cheesecake. Return the cheesecake to the oven for 10 minutes. Place on a rack to cool, then refrigerate until cold. Run a knife around the edge of the pan to loosen the spring pan sides and place on a large serving plate.

YIELD: *12 servings* EACH SERVING CONTAINS: *Carbohydrates:* 7 grams *Calories:* 49

Note: You can make yogurt cheese by placing yogurt in a strainer lined with cheesecloth set over a bowl to catch the liquid. Place in the refrigerator overnight to strain.

creamy amaretto cheesecake

My taste-testers loved this almond-flavored cheesecake. You can substitute lowfat cream cheese if you want to cut down on the fat and calories.

2 (8-ounce) packages cream cheese
2 tablespoons cornstarch
2 teaspoons sugar substitute
2 tablespoons granulated sugar
¼ cup Amaretto
1 teaspoon vanilla extract
½ cup eggs or egg substitute
1 prepared 8-inch graham cracker crust (optional)
Fresh berries, for serving (optional)

Preheat the oven to 325°F. If you're not using the graham cracker crust, spray an 8-inch springform or other pie pan with nonstick cooking spray. Using an electric mixer at medium speed, cream the cream cheese, cornstarch, sugar substitute, sugar, Amaretto, and vanilla together in a large bowl. Add the eggs and beat until creamy.

Pour the batter into the graham cracker crust or prepared pan. Bake for 35 minutes, or until firm to the touch. (It will jiggle slightly, but will set during chilling). Place on a rack to cool, then refrigerate until cold. To remove from the springform pan, run a knife around the edge of the pan to loosen the cheesecake and remove from the pan onto a large plate. Serve, topped with berries, if desired.

YIELD: *8 servings* EACH SERVING (WITHOUT THE CRUST) CONTAINS: *Carbohydrates:* 7 grams *Calories:* 108

strawberry cream cheese tarts

These tarts are very light and fluffy and have a wonderful rich flavor. No one will guess they aren't loaded with fat and calories.

 6 ounces fat-free cream cheese
 ¾ cup fat-free cottage cheese
 ⅔ cup fat-free sour cream
 3 large eggs, separated
 7 teaspoons fructose
 1 recipe graham cracker crust
 Strawberry Topping (page 129), for serving

To prepare the filling, beat the cream cheese, cottage cheese, sour cream, egg yolks, and fructose together in a large bowl until smooth. In another bowl, beat the egg whites until soft peaks form and then fold them into the cheese mixture. Spoon the filling into the prepared crusts and chill until set. Top with Strawberry Topping.

YIELD: *18 tarts* EACH TART CONTAINS: *Carbohydrates: 6 grams Calories: 44*

graham cracker crust

 1⅔ cup graham cracker crumbs (about 22 squares crushed)
 3 packages sugar substitute
 6 tablespoons melted butter

Combine all ingredients in a medium bowl. Firmly press the crumb mixture in a thin layer in 16 small ramekins.

cheese flan

Y ou'll love serving this elegant dessert. It rivals desserts you'll find in fancy restaurants, yet it's easy to make, virtually foolproof, and low in carbs.

4 large eggs or equivalent egg substitute
½ cup fat-free sour cream
1 cup fat-free cream cheese
¼ cup fresh lemon juice
2 teaspoons vanilla extract
1 packet sugar substitute
Dash of nutmeg
4 tablespoons chopped walnuts
2 tablespoons measures-like-sugar sugar substitute
1 prepared 9-inch unbaked pie crust

Preheat the oven to 375°F. Spread the crust on the bottom of a flan pan or quiche dish.

Place the eggs, sour cream, cream cheese, lemon juice, vanilla, sugar substitute, and nutmeg into a blender and blend until smooth. Pour the mixture into the prepared pan or prepared pie crust, if desired. Bake for 25 minutes. Meanwhile, combine the walnuts and sugar substitute in a small bowl. Remove the flan from the oven, sprinkle the walnut mixture on top, and set on a rack to cool. Place the flan in the refrigerator to chill before serving.

YIELD: *16 servings* EACH SERVING CONTAINS: *Carbohydrates:* 6 grams *Calories:* 41

fruit tart

A tart has three parts: a delicate tart crust, a creamy filling, and a fruit topping. Although tarts look and taste spectacular, they are not difficult to make. You can make this in the morning and serve after dinner.

LIGHT TART CRUST

½ cup Wondra® flour

¼ teaspoon baking powder

¼ cup egg substitute

1 teaspoon granulated sugar

6 packets sugar substitute

1 teaspoon vanilla extract

1 tablespoon margarine or butter, melted

VANILLA TART FILLING

1½ teaspoons all-purpose flour

1 tablespoon cornstarch

2 packets plus 1 teaspoon sugar substitute

¼ cup egg substitute

½ cup skim milk

1 teaspoon vanilla extract

TOPPING

1 cup fresh raspberries

⅔ cup fresh blueberries

To make the crust, coat a 9-inch springform pan with cooking spray. Combine the flour and baking powder in a large bowl. In a separate bowl, use an electric mixer to beat the egg substitute, sugar, sugar substitute, and vanilla together for a full 3 minutes. Add the margarine and the flour mixture and beat until well incorporated.

Spoon the mixture evenly onto the bottom of the springform pan, spreading the dough evenly with a rubber spatula. Push the dough down firmly and spread it as if you were painting a flat surface.

Place the pan on a cookie sheet and bake it in a preheated 325°F oven for 20 minutes. Take the cookie sheet and pan out of the oven. Remove the side from the springform. Then remove the crust of its base and place onto a rack. Move the rack and crust back onto the cookie sheet and bake it an additional 20 minutes. Cool.

To make the filling, in the bowl of an electric mixer, combine the flour, cornstarch, and 2 packets of the sugar substitute. Add the egg substitute and beat for 2 minutes. Place the milk in a small saucepan over medium heat and bring to the boiling point, then turn off the heat. Slowly pour the hot milk into the flour mixture and beat briefly to combine. Pour the mixture back into the saucepan and cook for several minutes over medium heat, whisking constantly. When the mixture has thickened, turn off the heat. Stir in the vanilla and remaining 1 teaspoon sugar substitute.

Spread the filling over the tart crust. Then decorate with the raspberries and blueberries, placing a ring of raspberries all around the outside edge, followed by a ring of blueberries inside, repeating until you have about 6 rings of blueberries. Fill in the center with raspberries.

YIELD: *8 servings* EACH SERVING CONTAINS: *Carbohydrates:* 6 grams *Calories:* 78

swiss pear tart

T he first time I made this tart, I set it to cool and left the house to run an errand. When I came home, serious inroads had been made in tart consumption.

1¼ cups unsweetened applesauce
13 ounces pear halves in juice, drained and sliced
⅓ cup granulated sugar
1 cup dry white wine
Juice of half a lemon (about 3 tablespoons)
Pinch of ground cinnamon
Pinch of ground cloves
2 tablespoons cornstarch
2 tablespoons water
2 tablespoons all-fruit raspberry jam
8 tablespoons frozen lowfat non-dairy whipped topping, thawed (optional)
1 10-inch prepared pie crust

Preheat oven to 425°F. Puree the applesauce and half of the pears in a blender or food processor. Pour the mixture into a large saucepan and add the sugar, wine, lemon juice, cinnamon, and cloves. Blend the cornstarch and water together in a teacup until the cornstarch dissolves. Add the cornstarch to the applesauce mixture and stir well. Place over medium heat and cook at just below boiling, stirring frequently, until reduced to a thick puree, about 3 to 5 minutes. Remove from the heat and cool.

Pour the puree into the prepared pie crust and bake for 30 minutes, or until firm. Remove from the oven and arrange the remaining pear slices on top. Bake for another 10 minutes, or until pears are steaming but not browned. Place on a cooling rack to cool slightly. Brush the top of the tart with jam. (If the jam does not brush on easily, warm it slightly.) Refrigerate until ready to serve. Top with whipped topping, if desired.

YIELD: *8 servings* EACH SERVING CONTAINS: *Carbohydrates:* 25 grams *Calories:* 117

cookies
and squares

rich lemon shorties

F or the calories and carbs, these shorties are delicious. The potato
flour works to provide a smooth texture.

THE BASE
½ cup fat-free cream cheese

½ cup unsalted butter or margarine

2 tablespoons granulated sugar

3 packages sugar substitute

2 cups all-purpose flour

½ cup potato flour

TOPPING
2 tablespoons freshly grated lemon peel

3 tablespoons granulated sugar, plus ½ teaspoon granulated sugar
(optional)

3 packages sugar substitute

3 large eggs or equivalent egg substitute

½ cup all-purpose flour

¾ teaspoon baking powder

3 tablespoons fresh lemon juice

To make the base, using an electric mixer, cream together the cream cheese,
butter, sugar, and sugar substitute. In another bowl, sift together the all-purpose
and potato flours. Add the flour mixture to the cream cheese mixture and mix
well. Using your hands, spread the mixture along the bottom of a 9-by-13-inch
lasagne pan. Refrigerate while you preheat the oven to 350°F.

Bake for 15 to 20 minutes, or until lightly browned. Cool on a wire rack.
Meanwhile, using an electric mixer, beat the lemon peel, 3 tablespoons sugar,
sugar substitute, and eggs in a large bowl until smooth and creamy. Sift the flour
and baking powder together into a small bowl. Fold the flour mixture into the
egg mixture. Stir in the lemon juice. Pour the mixture over the cooled base.

Bake again in the 350°F oven for 25 minutes. Cool on a wire rack. Cut into squares and sprinkle with the ½ teaspoon sugar, if desired.

YIELD: *30 squares* EACH SQUARE CONTAINS: *Carbohydrates:* 13 grams *Calories:* 95

mehren pletzlach

Atraditional Passover treat from Eastern Europe.

2 pounds carrots, shredded fine
¼ cup plus 1 tablespoon granulated sugar
1¾ teaspoon powdered ginger
2 tablespoons fresh lemon juice
1½ cups coarsely ground almonds (optional)

Place the carrots in a large saucepan and stir in the ¼ cup sugar. Barely cover with water and bring to a boil over high heat. Reduce the heat to very low and cook until the sugar is completely dissolved, about 3 minutes. Add the ginger and lemon juice and gently simmer, stirring often, until all the moisture has evaporated. This may take a few hours, depending on how moist the mixture is. Add the almonds, if desired. Sprinkle the remaining 1 tablespoon sugar on a work surface and spread the carrot mixture over the sugar to a ¾-inch thickness. Smooth with a rubber spatula and trim the edges. Cut into 40 squares and cool, then roll each square into a ball.

YIELD: *40 balls* EACH BALL CONTAINS: *Carbohydrates:* 4 grams *Calories:* 16

walnut roll-up cookies

These are very yummy, a must for a low-carb lifestyle.

1 package active dry yeast

¼ cup warm water

2 cups all-purpose flour

¼ cup plus 2 tablespoons unsalted butter or margarine, melted

1 large egg, lightly beaten, or equivalent egg substitute

6 tablespoons (3-ounce package) fat-free cream cheese

2 tablespoons granulated sugar

1 teaspoon grated orange peel

1 teaspoon orange extract

½ cup finely ground walnuts

Preheat the oven to 375°F. Coat a cookie sheet with nonstick vegetable cooking spray.

In a small bowl, combine the yeast and warm water. In a large bowl, combine the flour and butter. Beat in the egg. Add the yeast mixture and stir just until combined, to form a dough. On a lightly floured board, roll out the dough into two 13-by-9-inch rectangles. In a large bowl using an electric mixer, beat the cream cheese until light and fluffy. Add the sugar, orange peel, and orange extract and beat well. Spread half the cream cheese mixture over each dough rectangle. Sprinkle walnuts over the tops. Starting at the long side, roll up the rectangles, jelly-roll style. Place the rolls seam side down on the cookie sheet. Bake for 20 to 25 minutes, or until golden brown. Place on a wire rack to cool, then cut into 1-inch slices.

YIELD: *24 cookies* EACH COOKIE CONTAINS: *Carbohydrates:* 12 grams *Calories:* 83

no-bake
coconut surprise

T his is an easy treat to whip together, and it keeps well in the refrigerator.

1 (8-ounce) package fat-free cream cheese
1 packet sugar substitute
1 tablespoon chopped walnuts
1 teaspoon orange extract
¼ cup toasted flaked coconut

In a medium bowl, beat the cream cheese with the sugar substitute until light and fluffy. Add the walnut extract and orange extract. Using about ½ teaspoon of the mixture at a time, shape into 20 balls. Roll each ball in coconut, and place in the refrigerator to chill before serving.

YIELD: *20 cookies* EACH COOKIE CONTAINS: *Carbohydrates:* 1 gram *Calories:* 33

swedish gingersnaps

My father used to roll out cookies like these between wax paper to get them very, very thin. They are called *pepparkakor* in Swedish, and traditionally they are cut into the shape of stars and hearts.

⅓ cup molasses
1 teaspoon ground ginger
1 teaspoon ground cinnamon
½ teaspoon ground cloves
6 packets sugar substitute
¾ tablespoon baking soda
⅔ cup margarine or unsalted butter
⅔ cup nonfat sour cream
¼ cup egg substitute or 1 large egg
5 cups all-purpose flour, sifted

Preheat the oven to 350°F. Coat a cookie sheet with nonstick cooking spray.

Place the molasses, ginger, cinnamon, and cloves in a large saucepan over high heat and bring to a boil. Remove from the heat and add the sugar substitute, baking soda, and margarine. Stir until the margarine melts. Add the sour cream, egg substitute, and flour and mix thoroughly. Turn out onto lightly floured board and knead into a ball. Wrap in plastic wrap and refrigerate for at least 2 hours. Roll a manageable amount of dough on a lightly floured board to a thickness of ¼-inch and cut with cookie cutters. Place on the cookie sheet and bake for 8 to 10 minutes, or until edges are lightly browned. Transfer to wire rack to cool.

YIELD: *250 very thin cookies* EACH COOKIE CONTAINS: *Carbohydrates:* 3 grams *Calories:* 13

dream cookies

An old fashioned cookie adapted for low-carb eating.

½ cup margarine or unsalted butter
¼ cup granulated sugar
6 packets sugar substitute
½ cup fat-free cream cheese
2 teaspoons vanilla extract
1 teaspoon baking powder
2 cups all-purpose flour, sifted
20 blanched almonds, halved

Preheat the oven to 250°F. Coat a cookie sheet with nonstick cooking spray.

Brown the margarine slightly in a frying pan placed over medium-high heat. Let cool and transfer to a large bowl. Add the sugar, sugar substitute, and cream cheese and beat until smooth and well blended. Add the vanilla and baking powder and mix well. Add the flour and mix again. The dough will be crumbly.

Using your hands, roll the dough into smooth balls about the size of walnuts. Place on the cookie sheet and nestle an almond half into the top of each ball. Bake about 30 minutes, or until golden brown. Transfer to wire rack to cool.

YIELD: *40 cookies* EACH COOKIE CONTAINS: *Carbohydrates:* 7 grams *Calories:* 51

thumbprint cookies

Cute and yummy, and one of the easiest recipes in this book to make.

1 large egg or equivalent egg substitute
2 tablespoons skim milk
1½ cups all-purpose flour
2 tablespoons granulated sugar
3 packets sugar substitute
2 teaspoons baking powder
½ cup margarine or unsalted butter, softened
1 teaspoon vanilla extract
2 tablespoons seedless all-fruit raspberry or strawberry jam

Preheat the oven to 350°F. In a large bowl, beat together the egg and milk. Remove 1 tablespoon and set it aside in a small bowl to be used later. Sift together the flour, sugar, sugar substitute, and baking powder into a large bowl. Add the flour mixture, margarine, and vanilla to the egg mixture and mix until thoroughly blended.

Roll into balls the size of walnuts and place them on ungreased cookie sheets. Press a thumbprint into the top of each cookie and fill with jam. Brush the cookies with the egg and milk mixture. Bake for 10 to 15 minutes, or until golden brown. Transfer to wire rack to cool.

YIELD: *42 cookies* EACH COOKIE CONTAINS: *Carbohydrates:* 7 grams *Calories:* 45

almond rusks

This is a traditional Scandinavian rusk, very like the Italian version, biscotti. You make and bake a cake, cut it into fingers, and then toast the fingers until they are crunchy. They are great served with coffee or a frozen dessert or even with gelatin.

½ cup margarine or unsalted butter
¼ cup granulated sugar
3 packets sugar substitute
2 tablespoons fat-free sour cream
2 large eggs, lightly beaten, or equivalent egg substitute
1 teaspoon almond extract
2 cups all-purpose flour
2 teaspoons baking powder
1 cup finely chopped blanched almonds

Preheat the oven to 350°F. Cream the margarine, sugar, sugar substitute, and sour cream together in a large bowl. Add the eggs and almond extract and stir well. Add the flour, baking powder, and almonds and stir well. Spread the batter over an 8½-inch square cake pan. Bake for 25 minutes, or until a cake tester inserted into the center comes out clean. The center springs back when tested. Remove to a cooling rack and cool thoroughly. To make the rusks, slice the cake in half horizontally, then slice each half into fingers that are ¾ inches long by 2 inches wide. Lay the rusks on an ungreased cookie sheet cut side up and bake for 10 minutes, or until lightly browned. Transfer to a wire rack to cool.

YIELD: *64 rusks* EACH RUSK CONTAINS: *Carbohydrates:* 2 grams *Calories:* 43

sweet potato cookies

These are very moist, soft cookies. You can make them with canned sweet potatoes—just drain them well first.

¼ cup granulated sugar
3 packets sugar substitute
¼ cup fat-free cream cheese
1 cup cooked and mashed sweet potatoes
¼ cup margarine or unsalted butter
1 egg or equivalent egg substitute
2 cups rolled oats
1 teaspoon ground cinnamon
½ teaspoon baking soda
¼ teaspoon ground cloves
1 apple, peeled, cored, and chopped fine

Preheat the oven to 350°F. Coat a cookie sheet with nonstick cooking spray. Beat together the sugar, sugar substitute, and cream cheese in a large bowl until smooth. Add the remaining ingredients except the chopped apple and beat well, then gently stir in the apple.

Drop the batter by the tablespoon onto the cookie sheet. Using the back of a spoon, press each cookie into a patty. Bake for 15 to 20 minutes, or until lightly browned. Place the cookies on a wire rack to cool.

YIELD: *50 cookies* EACH COOKIE CONTAINS: *Carbohydrates:* 3 grams *Calories:* 23

piña colada squares

There is something about the piña colada taste and texture that's so tropical. You can pour this treat into dessert or wine glasses before chilling for a special presentation.

4 envelopes unflavored gelatin
6 packages sugar substitute
2½ cups unsweetened pineapple juice
1 cup frozen lowfat non-dairy whipped topping, thawed
1 teaspoon coconut extract
½ teaspoon rum extract

Coat an 8-inch square pan with nonstick cooking spray. Place the gelatin and sugar substitute into a large bowl. Stir in ½ cup of the pineapple juice. Set aside. Meanwhile, in a small saucepan over medium heat, bring the remaining 2 cups pineapple juice to a boil. Add the hot pineapple juice all at once to the gelatin mixture, stirring to combine. Stir in the whipped topping and coconut and rum extract. Pour the batter into the pan and place in the refrigerator to chill until firm. Cut into 9 squares.

YIELD: *9 squares* EACH SQUARE CONTAINS: *Carbohydrates:* 18 grams *Calories:* 99

walnut spice kisses

This meringue cookie is so easy to make. When the weather is damp, meringue tends to be sticky, so the cookies tend to be chewy in damp weather and crisp when the humidity is low.

1 large egg white
2 dashes of salt
2 tablespoons granulated sugar
2 packets sugar substitute
1 teaspoon ground cinnamon
⅛ teaspoon ground nutmeg
⅛ teaspoon ground cloves
1 cup finely chopped walnuts
30 walnut halves

Preheat the oven to 250°F. Coat a cookie sheet with nonstick cooking spray.

In a large bowl, using an electric mixer, beat the egg white until stiff peaks form. Gradually beat in the salt. In another bowl, combine the sugar, sugar substitute, cinnamon, nutmeg, and cloves. Beat the dry ingredients into the egg white. Fold in the chopped walnuts.

Drop by the teaspoon onto the cookie sheet. Top each cookie with a walnut half. Bake for 35 to 40 minutes. Do not brown. Transfer to a wire rack to cool.

YIELD: *30 cookies* EACH COOKIE CONTAINS: *Carbohydrates:* 3 grams *Calories:* 32

rice krispies-and-date squares

These are yummy beyond belief. *Hint:* Use a sharp, wet knife to cut the dates.

- ¾ cup chopped dates
- 2 tablespoons margarine
- 1 egg, slightly beaten, or equivalent egg substitute
- 1 tablespoon fat-free milk
- 1 teaspoon vanilla extract
- 4 packets sugar substitute
- 3 cups plain toasted rice cereal

Coat an 8-inch square pan with nonstick cooking spray.

Combine the dates, margarine, egg, milk, and vanilla in a medium saucepan over medium heat. Cook until thickened, about 5 minutes. Remove from the heat to cool, then stir in the sugar substitute and rice cereal. Press into the pan and refrigerate until firm. Cut into 24 squares.

YIELD: *24 squares* EACH SQUARE CONTAINS: *Carbohydrates:* 8 grams *Calories:* 36

apple squares

These squares travel well and are moist and delicious, so they are great to take to work. In addition, they are quick and easy to make—the hard part is waiting for them to cool before eating them.

6 packets sugar substitute
1 cup all-purpose flour
1 teaspoon baking soda
1 teaspoon ground cinnamon
1 large egg or equivalent egg substitute
¼ cup canola oil
2 teaspoons vanilla extract
2 cups peeled, cored, and chopped apples
2 tablespoons water

Preheat the oven to 350°F. Coat an 8-inch square pan with nonstick cooking spray.

Sift together the sugar substitute, flour, baking soda, and cinnamon into a large bowl. Combine the egg, oil, and vanilla in a separate bowl. Add to the flour mixture. Using an electric mixer, set at medium speed, beat until well blended and stiff. Add the apples and water and mix well. Turn into the pan and bake for 25 minutes, or until a toothpick inserted in the center comes out clean. Place the pan on a rack to cool for 10 minutes, then cut into 24 2 x 1⅓-inch slices.

YIELD: *24 squares* EACH SQUARE CONTAINS: *Carbohydrates:* 15 grams *Calories:* 69

café au lait squares

This recipe is adapted from one of my grandmother's. It's terrific with flavored coffees, such as vanilla and hazelnut. For a special presentation prepare these in your best coffee cups instead of a pan.

4 envelopes unflavored gelatin
1 cup skim milk
1½ cups strong-brewed coffee
6 tablespoons semisweet chocolate chips (use lowfat chips, if available)
6 packages sugar substitute
1½ teaspoons vanilla extract

Coat an 8-inch square baking pan with nonstick cooking spray.

Place the gelatin in a medium bowl. Stir in the milk and set aside. In a small saucepan over medium heat, bring the coffee to a boil. Pour the coffee over the gelatin and stir until the gelatin is completely dissolved. Stir in the chocolate chips, sugar substitute, and vanilla. Pour the batter into the pan. Place in the refrigerator to chill until firm. Cut into 9 2½-inch squares.

YIELD: *9 squares* EACH SQUARE CONTAINS: *Carbohydrates:* 9 grams *Calories:* 81

langues-de-chat

My grandmother used to serve these with coffee on her sun porch on summer afternoons. I've made some changes to the recipe, but its wonderful rich character remains.

2 tablespoons unsalted butter or margarine

2 tablespoons fat-free cream cheese

3 packages sugar substitute

3 tablespoons granulated sugar

1 large egg, lightly beaten or equivalent egg substitute

1 teaspoon vanilla extract

¼ teaspoon butter-flavored extract

½ cup all-purpose flour, sifted

Preheat the oven to 425°F. Grease 2 baking sheets and line with parchment or wax paper. In a medium bowl, beat the butter, cream cheese, sugar substitute, and sugar together until light and fluffy. Slowly beat in the egg and vanilla and butter-flavored extracts. Fold in the flour to form a soft dough.

Spoon the dough carefully into a pastry bag fitted with a ⅜-inch plain tip. Squeeze out into 3-inch lengths onto the baking sheets, cutting off the dough with a sharp knife after each one. Bake for 8 to 10 minutes, or until the edges are lightly browned. Place the sheets on wire racks to cool before removing the cookies.

YIELD: *30 cookies*   EACH COOKIE CONTAINS: *Carbohydrates:* 3 grams *Calories:* 23

cream cheese cookies

Without the fat-free dairy products, this recipe would never have been possible.

4 tablespoons unsalted butter or margarine
1 cup fat-free cream cheese
2 tablespoons granulated sugar
4 packages sugar substitute
1 large egg, lightly beaten or equivalent egg substitute
1½ cups all-purpose flour
1 teaspoon baking powder
½ teaspoon butter-flavored extract
½ cup fat-free sour cream

Preheat the oven to 400°F.

Cream the butter and cream cheese together in a large bowl until soft and creamy. Blend in the sugar and sugar substitute, then blend in the egg. In a medium bowl, sift together the flour and baking powder. In a small bowl, combine the butter-flavored extract and sour cream. Alternately add the flour mixture and the sour cream mixture to the butter and cream cheese mixture, blending thoroughly.

Form the dough into a ball and wrap it in plastic wrap. Refrigerate until chilled. Roll out the dough on a lightly floured board until it is about ⅛-inch thick. Use cookie cutters to cut out the dough. Place cookies on a baking sheet and bake cookies for 8 to 10 minutes, or until slightly browned around the edges. Cool cookies on a wire rack.

YIELD: *90 small cookies* EACH COOKIE CONTAINS: *Carbohydrates:* 2 grams *Calories:* 17

pies
and tortes

pumpkin-apple pie

Everyone will want seconds when you serve this pie. Topping it with frozen whipped topping or low-carb vanilla ice cream makes for a fancy dessert.

⅓ cup unsweetened apple juice
1 tablespoon cornstarch
1 teaspoon ground cinnamon
1 teaspoon rum-flavored extract
3 cups peeled, cored, and sliced apples (3 medium or 2 large apples)
1 large egg or equivalent egg substitute
¾ cup canned or cooked mashed pumpkin
¼ teaspoon ground ginger
⅛ teaspoon ground cloves
⅓ cup measures-like-sugar sugar substitute
¾ cup evaporated skim milk
1 (9-inch) frozen pie crust
Frozen lowfat non-dairy whipped topping, thawed, or low-carb vanilla
    ice cream, for serving (optional)

Preheat the oven to 375°F. Combine the apple juice, cornstarch, ½ teaspoon of the cinnamon, and the rum-flavored extract in a large saucepan over medium heat. Bring to a boil, stirring constantly. Add the apples and cook for 4 minutes, stirring constantly, until well mixed and thickened.

In a large bowl, beat the eggs, then add the pumpkin, ginger, remaining ½ teaspoon cinnamon, the cloves, sugar substitute, and evaporated skim milk. Stir to blend well.

Turn the apple mixture into the prepared pie crust. Spread the pumpkin mixture on top. Bake for 30 minutes, or until the pumpkin is set and very lightly browned. Cool on a wire rack.

Top with whipped topping or low-carb vanilla ice cream, if desired.

YIELD: *8 servings* EACH SERVING CONTAINS: *Carbohydrates:* 15 grams *Calories:* 132

lemon meringue torte

T his special torte has meringue on both the bottom and the top.

1 recipe Basic Meringue (page 153)
1 package (4 servings) sugar-free lemon pudding mix
1¼ cups water or skim milk
2 teaspoons fresh lemon juice

Preheat the oven to 250°F. Prepare the Basic Meringue recipe. Cut brown paper bags or parchment paper to fit over 2 cookie sheets. Trace 2 dinner plates on the paper. Spoon the meringue into the 2 circles, smoothing it evenly.

Bake for 1 hour. Turn off the oven but do not open the door. Leave in the oven for an additional 30 minutes, then remove to wire racks to cool.

Use a spatula to remove the torte shells from the paper. Prepare the lemon pudding according to the package directions, using water or skim milk. Stir in the lemon juice. Place one of the meringues on a serving plate just before you are ready to serve. Scoop half of the lemon mixture on top of the meringue. Top with the second meringue. Decorate the top with dollops of the remaining pudding. Cut with a sharp wet knife.

YIELD: *8 servings* EACH SERVING CONTAINS: *Carbohydrates:* 7 grams *Calories:* 33

blueberry-yogurt pie

Thisis a substantial pie that's great after a light dinner.

- 1 tablespoon unflavored gelatin
- ¼ cup water
- 2 large egg yolks, lightly beaten
- 1 cup fat-free cottage cheese
- 1 cup lowfat blueberry yogurt
- 1 cup frozen lowfat non-dairy whipped topping, thawed, plus more for serving (optional)
- 4 teaspoons sugar substitute
- 1 (10-inch) frozen pie crust, baked
- ½ cup fresh or frozen and thawed unsweetened blueberries

Combine the gelatin and water in a small saucepan and let stand for a few minutes to soften. Add the egg yolks. Place over low heat and cook, stirring constantly, until the mixture begins to thicken. Remove from the heat and set aside. Place the cottage cheese in a large bowl and stir in the gelatin mixture. Add the yogurt, whipped topping, and sugar substitute, stirring well after each addition.

Turn the mixture into the pie crust. Refrigerate for 6 to 8 hours before serving. Top with the blueberries and additional whipped topping, if desired.

YIELD: *8 servings* EACH SERVING CONTAINS: *Carbohydrates:* 19 grams *Calories:* 170

double blueberry pie

This recipe uses both cooked and fresh blueberries, which makes for great flavor and texture.

6 ounces (¾ cup) fat-free cream cheese
2 tablespoons skim milk
½ teaspoon lemon extract
4 cups fresh or frozen and thawed unsweetened blueberries
1 tablespoon fresh lemon juice
2 tablespoons cornstarch
7 tablespoons sugar substitute
1 (9-inch) frozen pie crust, baked
Frozen lowfat non-dairy whipped topping, thawed,
    for serving (optional)

Place the cream cheese in a large bowl. Add the milk and lemon extract. Using an electric mixer on medium speed, whip until smooth and soft. Coat the bottom of the pie shell with the cream cheese mixture, taking care not to damage the shell.

Arrange 2 cups of the blueberries on top of the cream cheese. Mash the remaining 2 cups blueberries and put them into a 2-cup measure. Add the lemon juice to the blueberries and enough water so it reaches the 1½-cups mark. Transfer the mixture to a small saucepan. Add the cornstarch and stir to blend. Place the pan over medium heat and bring to a boil, stirring constantly. Cook for a minute or two, until the mixture is thick. Remove from the heat and set aside to cool to lukewarm, then stir in the sugar substitute.

Spoon the blueberry sauce over the pie. Refrigerate for at least 3 hours before serving. Serve with dollops of your favorite whipped topping, if desired.

YIELD: *8 servings* EACH SERVING CONTAINS: *Carbohydrates:* 23 grams *Calories:* 157

apricot cream pie

I recommend decorating the top with dried apricot slivers and fresh mint leaves.

2 large egg yolks, lightly beaten
1½ cups unsweetened apricot nectar
1 envelope unflavored gelatin
1 tablespoon lemon juice (fresh is best)
2 cups frozen lowfat non-dairy whipped topping, thawed
1 (9-inch) frozen pie crust, baked

Place the egg yolks and apricot nectar in a medium saucepan and whisk together. Place over medium heat and cook, stirring constantly, until slightly thickened. Remove from the heat.

In a small bowl, combine the gelatin and lemon juice. Stir and let sit for a minute or two, then add to the hot liquid. Stir. Cool for 15 to 20 minutes, then pour into a large bowl. Stir in the whipped topping, then pour into the prepared pie crust. Refrigerate for 3 to 4 hours, or until set, before serving.

YIELD: *8 servings* EACH SERVING CONTAINS: *Carbohydrates:* 20 grams *Calories:* 165

lime chiffon pie

The "Parrot Heads" (Jimmy Buffett fans) around my house think this is a great low-carb substitute for Key lime pie.

1 package (4 servings) sugar-free lime gelatin mix
½ cup boiling water
1 tablespoon lime juice (Key lime is best)
½ cup cold water
Ice cubes
2 cups frozen lowfat non-dairy whipped topping, thawed
1 (9-inch) frozen pie crust, baked

Place the gelatin in a large bowl. Add the boiling water and stir until the gelatin is dissolved. Add the lime juice. Put the cold water into a 1-cup measuring cup and add enough ice cubes to reach the 1-cup mark. Pour the water and ice mixture into a blender or food processor. Add the gelatin mixture and blend until the ice has been incorporated. Add the whipped topping and blend again to mix. Spoon into the prepared pie crust. Refrigerate at least 1 hour before serving.

YIELD: *8 servings* EACH SERVING CONTAINS: *Carbohydrates:* 13 grams *Calories:* 124

lemon chiffon pie

This is a great way to end a meal that features a fish entrée.

Prepare the Lime Chiffon Pie above, but substitute lemon gelatin for the lime and lemon juice for the lime juice.

YIELD: *8 servings* EACH SERVING CONTAINS: *Carbohydrates:* 13 grams *Calories:* 124

raspberry shimmer pie

This layered pie looks and tastes spectacular. Don't be overwhelmed by the length of the directions—there's nothing tricky to it.

4 cups fresh or frozen unsweetened raspberries
1 cup water
3 tablespoons cornstarch
2 teaspoons fresh lemon juice
7 teaspoons sugar substitute
6 tablespoons fat-free cream cheese
1 tablespoon skim milk
1 (9-inch) frozen pie crust, baked
Frozen lowfat non-dairy whipped topping, thawed, or
  low-carb ice cream, for serving (optional)

Place 1 cup of the raspberries and ⅔ cup of the water in a small saucepan over medium heat. Bring to a simmer and cook for 3 to 4 minutes, or until well heated. Pour the mixture through a fine strainer to remove the seeds. Return the liquid to the saucepan. Stir in the remaining ⅓ cup water and the cornstarch. Cook, stirring constantly, until the mixture is thick. Stir in the lemon juice. Set aside to cool, then add the sugar substitute and mix thoroughly.

Place the cream cheese in a medium bowl and add the milk. Using an electric mixer, whip until soft. Spread the cream cheese mixture very gently over the bottom of the pie crust, taking care not to damage the crust. Spread most of the reserved berries (saving a few for garnish) over the cream cheese mixture. Spread the cooked berry mixture over the fresh berries. Refrigerate for 2 to 3 hours. Serve with your favorite low-carb whipped topping or low-carb ice cream, if desired, and garnish with the reserved raspberries.

YIELD: *8 servings* EACH SERVING CONTAINS: *Carbohydrates:* 20 grams *Calories:* 140

raspberry ribbon pie

T he ribbon in the title refers to this unique pie's red and white layers.

1 package (4 servings) sugar-free raspberry gelatin mix

1¼ cups boiling water

10 ounces frozen unsweetened whole red raspberries

1 tablespoon fresh lemon juice

6 tablespoons (3 ounces) fat-free cream cheese

2 teaspoons sugar substitute

1 teaspoon vanilla extract

1 cup frozen lowfat non-dairy whipped topping, thawed

1 (9-inch) frozen pie crust, baked

To prepare the red layers, place the gelatin in a large bowl and add the boiling water. Add the raspberries and lemon juice and stir until the raspberries are defrosted. Refrigerate for 1 to 2 hours, until partially set.

To prepare the white layers, in a medium bowl, combine the cream cheese, sugar substitute, and vanilla. Fold in a spoonful of the whipped topping. Continue to fold in the topping, a spoonful at a time. Refrigerate until the white layer is partially set, about 30 minutes.

Spread one third of the white mixture on the bottom of the prepared pie crust. Cover with half of the red gelatin mixture. Repeat with white and red layers, ending with the white mixture. Chill until set, at least 3 hours, before serving.

YIELD: *8 servings* EACH SERVING CONTAINS: *Carbohydrates:* 16 grams *Calories:* 132

raspberry cream pie

Prepare this in the morning and leave it to freeze all day.

1 (4 servings) package sugar-free raspberry gelatin mix
⅔ cup boiling water
1½ cups sugar-free lowfat vanilla ice cream
1½ cups frozen lowfat non-dairy whipped topping, thawed
1 cup fresh or frozen and thawed unsweetened whole raspberries
1 (9-inch) frozen pie crust, baked

Place the gelatin in a large bowl. Add the boiling water and stir until the gelatin is dissolved. Slowly add the ice cream and stir until the mixture is smooth. Stir in the whipped topping until well blended. Add the raspberries, saving a few for garnishing.

Spread the mixture over the prepared pie crust. Freeze until firm, at least an hour. To slice, run a sharp knife under hot running water after each cut. Top each slice with a dollop of whipped topping and raspberries.

YIELD: *8 servings* EACH SERVING CONTAINS: *Carbohydrates:* 18 grams *Calories:* 140

hawaiian pineapple pie

I don't think I was ever served this in Hawaii, but it does bring out the spirit of the islands.

20 ounces canned unsweetened crushed pineapple in juice
1 package (4 servings) sugar-free vanilla pudding mix
½ cup water
1 teaspoon unsalted butter or margarine
1 (9-inch) frozen pie crust, baked
½ cup frozen lowfat non-dairy whipped topping, thawed
2 tablespoons unsweetened coconut flakes (optional)

Drain the crushed pineapple, reserving the juice. In a medium saucepan, combine the pudding mix, water, and reserved pineapple juice. Place over medium heat, stirring constantly. When the mixture comes to a full boil, add the crushed pineapple and butter. Stir well.

Pour the filling into the pie crust and let cool in the refrigerator. Just before serving, top with the whipped topping and sprinkle with the coconut flakes, if desired.

YIELD: *8 servings* EACH SERVING CONTAINS: *Carbohydrates:* 21 grams *Calories:* 140

peach cream cheese pie

T his pie is not too sweet—it's perfect after dinner on a hot summer evening.

½ cup orange juice
2 envelopes unflavored gelatin
2 teaspoons orange extract
1 cup fat-free cream cheese
1 cup frozen lowfat non-dairy whipped topping, thawed
16 ounces lite peach slices in juice, drained and chopped
1 (9-inch) frozen pie crust, baked

In a small saucepan over medium heat, heat the orange juice until simmering. Pour into a blender or food processor and add the gelatin and orange extract. Blend for about 30 seconds, then add the cream cheese, whipped topping, and peach slices. Blend for about another 20 seconds, until smooth.

Quickly pour the filling into the pie crust. Refrigerate for at least 3 hours before serving.

YIELD: *8 servings* EACH SERVING CONTAINS: *Carbohydrates:* 22 grams *Calories:* 170

strawberry ice cream pie

Take the ice cream out of the freezer to soften before beginning this recipe. An old-fashioned treat after dinner on a warm evening or a luscious dessert with a salad lunch.

1 package (4 servings) sugar-free strawberry gelatin mix
⅔ cup boiling water
2 cups sugar-free lowfat strawberry ice cream, softened
1 cup frozen lowfat non-dairy whipped topping, thawed, plus more
    for serving (optional)
1 (9-inch) frozen pie crust, baked
Fresh strawberries for serving (optional)

Place the gelatin in a large bowl. Add the boiling water and stir until the gelatin is dissolved. Slowly add the ice cream and stir until the mixture is smooth (except for the strawberry pieces, of course). Stir in the whipped topping by spoonfuls, beating with a whisk after each addition.

Spoon the mixture into the prepared pie crust. Freeze for a few hours until firm. To slice, run a sharp knife under hot running water after each cut. Garnish with strawberries and whipped topping, if desired.

YIELD: *8 servings* EACH SERVING CONTAINS: *Carbohydrates:* 17 grams *Calories:* 128

banana cream and strawberry pie

Bananas and strawberries make a delightful taste combination here.

1 package (4 servings) sugar-free strawberry-banana gelatin mix
⅔ cup boiling water
2 cups sugar-free lowfat vanilla ice cream, softened
1 cup frozen lowfat non-dairy whipped topping, thawed
1 (9-inch) frozen pie crust, baked
1 medium banana, sliced
1 cup sliced fresh strawberries

Place the gelatin in a large bowl. Add the boiling water and stir until the gelatin is dissolved. Slowly add the ice cream and stir until smooth. Stir in the whipped topping by spoonfuls, beating after each addition.

Spoon the mixture into the prepared pie crust, smoothing the top with a spoon. Freeze for at least 1 hour, until firm. To slice, run a sharp knife under hot running water after each cut. Just before serving, combine the banana and strawberry slices and spoon them over the pie slices.

YIELD: *8 servings* EACH SERVING CONTAINS: *Carbohydrates:* 22 grams *Calories:* 147

strawberry
cream cheese pie

The cream cheese here makes for a low-carb pie with a smooth and rich consistency.

1 cup fat-free cream cheese
¼ cup all-fruit strawberry jam
½ teaspoon almond extract or 1 tablespoon almond-flavored liqueur
1 cup frozen lowfat non-dairy whipped topping, thawed
1 (9-inch) frozen pie crust, baked
2 cups fresh or frozen unsweetened strawberries

Using an electric mixer set at medium speed, beat together the cream cheese, jam, and almond extract. Reduce the speed to low and beat in the whipped topping until smooth.

Spoon the mixture to the prepared pie crust, smoothing the top with a spoon. Top with the strawberries. Freeze for at least an hour before serving. To slice, run a sharp knife under hot running water after each cut.

YIELD: *8 servings* EACH SERVING CONTAINS: *Carbohydrates:* 19 grams *Calories:* 156

strawberry meringue pie

Dessert lovers will be delighted with the ice cream–meringue combination in this baked Alaska–style pie with strawberries. You can try it topped with one of the chocolate or mocha toppings if you like.

1 (9-inch) frozen pie crust, baked

4 cups sugar-free lowfat vanilla ice cream, softened

3 cups fresh or frozen and thawed unsweetened strawberries

2 large egg whites

¼ teaspoon cream of tartar

1½ teaspoons sugar substitute

Spread the ice cream over the pie crust, making sure it reaches the edges. Freeze all day or overnight. Just before serving, spread the strawberries on top of the ice cream and preheat the oven to 500°F. Place the egg whites, cream of tartar, and sugar substitute in the bowl of an electric mixer. Beat at high speed until the whites form stiff peaks but are not dry. Spoon the meringue on top of the strawberries, using a spoon to make decorative peaks. Make sure the entire surface is covered, right up to the crust.

Place the pie on a wooden breadboard or a cookie sheet and place it in the oven. Bake for about 5 minutes, or until the meringue is lightly browned. Serve immediately.

YIELD: *8 servings* EACH SERVING CONTAINS: *Carbohydrates:* 24 grams *Calories:* 150

pumpkin ice cream pie

I f you like pumpkin, you'll love this frozen ice cream pie. My mom enjoyed this cold and refreshing treat at Thanksgiving after a heavy meal.

2 cups sugar-free lowfat vanilla ice cream, softened
1 (9-inch) frozen pie crust, baked
5 teaspoons sugar substitute
½ teaspoon ground cinnamon
½ teaspoon ground ginger
¼ teaspoon ground nutmeg
1 cup canned pumpkin puree
1 cup frozen lowfat non-dairy whipped topping, thawed

Spread the softened ice cream over the bottom of the prepared pie crust, taking care not to damage the shell. Place in the freezer. In a large bowl, combine the sugar substitute, cinnamon, ginger, and nutmeg. Add the pumpkin and mix well. Fold in the whipped topping until well mixed.

Remove the pie crust from the freezer and spread the pumpkin mixture over the ice cream. Freeze for 2 to 3 hours. Remove from the freezer a half hour before slicing.

YIELD: *8 servings* EACH SERVING CONTAINS: *Carbohydrates:* 18 grams *Calories:* 136

butterscotch pie

Although this delicious pie is made with pumpkin, the butterscotch flavor is the dominant one.

1 tablespoon unflavored gelatin
1½ cups skim milk
6 tablespoons (3 ounces) fat-free cream cheese
1½ cups canned pumpkin pie filling
2 large eggs or equivalent egg substitute
1 package (4 servings) sugar-free butterscotch pudding mix
   (not instant)
2 cups frozen lowfat non-dairy whipped topping, thawed
1 (9-inch) frozen pie crust, baked

Place the gelatin in a small bowl. Stir in ½ cup of the milk. Set aside while the gelatin softens. In the bowl of an electric mixer, combine the cream cheese, pumpkin pie filling, and eggs and beat at medium speed until smooth.

In a heavy-bottomed saucepan over medium heat, combine the remaining 1 cup milk and the pudding mix. Add the pumpkin filling and gelatin and cook until the mixture bubbles and thickens, about 3 to 5 minutes. Put the pan in the refrigerator to cool for about 45 minutes, but do not allow it to set. Fold in the whipped topping.

Spoon the filling into the prepared pie crust. Chill for several hours or overnight before serving.

YIELD: *8 servings* EACH SERVING CONTAINS: *Carbohydrates:* 17 grams *Calories:* 179

chocolate chocolate pie

H ershey's low-sugar, no-fat chocolate syrup works very nicely in
this chocolate-packed recipe.

1¼ cups water or skim milk
2 packages (4 servings each) sugar-free chocolate pudding mix
1 (9-inch) frozen pie crust, baked
1½ cups fat-free cream cheese
2 tablespoons low-sugar fat-free chocolate syrup
1½ cups frozen lowfat non-dairy whipped topping, thawed

Using the water or milk, make the pudding following the package directions.
Turn the pudding into the pie crust. Place the cream cheese and 1 tablespoon
milk into a large bowl. Using an electric mixer, beat on high speed until
smooth. Using the lowest speed, beat in the chocolate syrup and whipped topping. Pour the cream cheese mixture into the pie crust over the pudding mixture. Refrigerate at least 3 hours before serving.

YIELD: *8 servings* EACH SERVING CONTAINS: *Carbohydrates:* 18 grams *Calories:* 151

coffee and cream pie

If coffee in a cup tasted this good, I'd drink a lot more of it. To cut the fat down to practically nothing, make it with fat-free whipped topping.

3 cups frozen lowfat non-dairy whipped topping, thawed
2 tablespoons instant coffee powder
1 teaspoon vanilla extract
¼ cup cold water
1 envelope unflavored gelatin
1 (9-inch) frozen pie crust, baked
½ cup unsweetened toasted coconut flakes (optional)

Place the whipped topping, coffee powder, and vanilla in a large bowl and beat until blended. Pour the cold water into a small saucepan and sprinkle the gelatin over the water. Let stand a minute or two, then put the saucepan over low heat and stir until the gelatin is thoroughly dissolved. Pour the gelatin into the coffee mixture and beat again, until the gelatin is blended in.

Pour the mixture into the prepared pie crust. Sprinkle the coconut over the top, if desired. Refrigerate at least 1 hour before serving.

YIELD: *8 servings* EACH SERVING CONTAINS: *Carbohydrates:* 15 grams *Calories:* 160

blueberry-sour cream pie

Both fresh and frozen blueberries will work equally well here.

2 cups fresh or frozen blueberries
1 (9-inch) unbaked frozen pie crust
1 cup fat-free sour cream
2 tablespoons granulated sugar
3 packages sugar substitute
1 large egg yolk, lightly beaten
1 teaspoon vanilla extract

Preheat the oven to 375°F.

Scatter the blueberries over the pie crust. Combine the remaining ingredients in a large bowl and pour over the blueberries.

Bake for 45 minutes, or until the top is lightly browned. Place on a rack to cool, then place in the refrigerator to chill before serving.

YIELD: *8 servings* EACH SERVING CONTAINS: *Carbohydrates:* 19 grams *Calories:* 143

quick custard pie

T his is great for cold winter nights. You can cut down on the fat by using egg substitute.

4 large eggs or equivalent egg substitute
3 tablespoons granulated sugar
6 packages sugar substitute
¼ teaspoon ground nutmeg
1 teaspoon vanilla extract
½ teaspoon butter-flavored extract
1 (9-inch) unbaked frozen pie crust

Preheat the oven to 350°F. Place all the ingredients (except the pie crust!) into a food processor or blender. Process until the sugar is dissolved and the mixture is well blended. Pour into the pie crust. Bake for 30 minutes, or until a knife inserted into the center of the pie comes out clean. Cool on a wire rack. Serve warm or refrigerate and serve cold.

YIELD: *8 servings* EACH SERVING CONTAINS: *Carbohydrates:* 16 grams *Calories:* 160

sour cream pie

You can serve this pie with raspberry or strawberry sauce.

2 large eggs or equivalent egg substitute
1 cup fat-free sour cream
½ cup raisins
2 tablespoons granulated sugar
6 packages sugar substitute
1½ teaspoons ground cinnamon
¼ cup finely chopped pecans (optional)
1 (9-inch) unbaked frozen pie crust

Preheat the oven to 450°F. Place all the ingredients except the pecans and pie crust in a food processor or blender. Process until well mixed, scraping down the sides a few times if necessary. Add the pecans, if desired, and pulse a few times to blend.

Pour the mixture into the pie crust. Bake for 15 minutes, then reduce the oven temperature to 350°F and bake an additional 30 minutes, or until the crust is golden brown. Cool on a wire rack. Serve warm or refrigerate and serve cold.

YIELD: *8 servings* EACH SERVING CONTAINS: *Carbohydrates:* 22 grams *Calories:* 163

cocoa chiffon pie

This pie needs at least eight hours to chill, so prepare it the night before you plan to serve it—it's worth planning ahead for!

1 envelope unflavored gelatin
3 tablespoons unsweetened cocoa powder
1¾ cups skim milk
1 teaspoon vanilla extract
1½ cups frozen lowfat non-dairy whipped topping, thawed
1½ teaspoons sugar substitute
1 (9-inch) frozen pie crust, baked

In a medium saucepan, combine the gelatin, cocoa, and milk. Let stand for 5 minutes. Place over low heat and cook, stirring with a wire whisk until the gelatin is dissolved, about 5 minutes. Remove from heat and stir in the vanilla. Transfer to a bowl and refrigerate while preparing the rest of the pie.

Combine the whipped topping and sugar substitute in a large bowl. Add the cocoa mixture and mix with an electric mixer at the lowest speed until blended.

Turn the filling into the prepared pie crust. Refrigerate at least 8 hours or overnight before serving.

YIELD: *8 servings* EACH SERVING CONTAINS: *Carbohydrates:* 16 grams *Calories:* 145

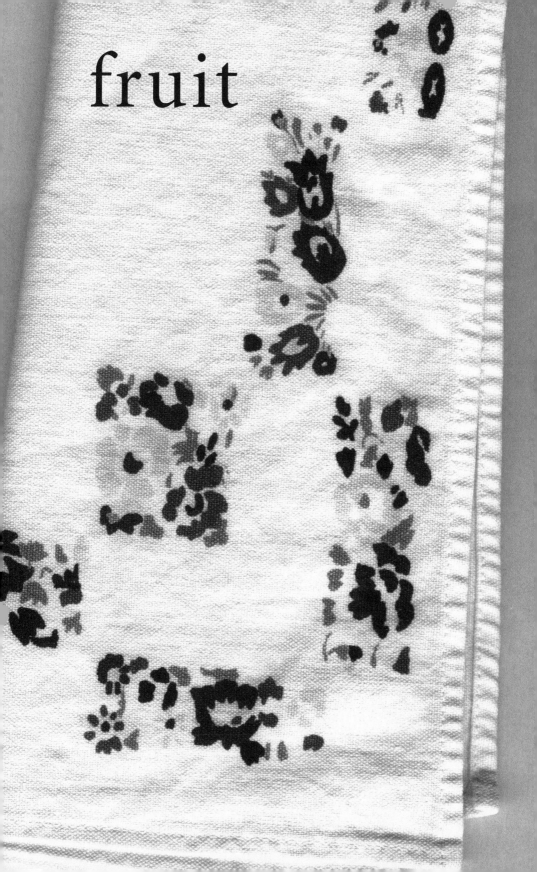

fruit

italian custard and berries

In place of the Marsala you can also try sherry or another flavored liqueur such as Amaretto.

2 tablespoons granulated sugar
2 teaspoons cornstarch
¾ cup 1% lowfat milk
1 large egg, beaten, or equivalent egg substitute
¼ cup fat-free sour cream
2 tablespoons Marsala
2 cups fresh berries
½ teaspoon ground cinnamon or nutmeg

In a small heavy saucepan, whisk together the sugar and cornstarch, then stir in the milk. Place over medium heat and cook, stirring constantly, for 2 minutes, or until thick and bubbly. Remove from heat. Pour the egg into a large bowl. Gradually pour in about half of the hot liquid, stirring constantly. Return the mixture to the saucepan. Cook until nearly boiling, but do not allow it to boil.

Pour into a serving bowl and stir in the sour cream and Marsala. Cover with plastic wrap and place in the refrigerator to chill for at least 2 hours before serving. Divide the berries among 4 individual dessert dishes, and spoon the custard over the berries. Sprinkle the tops with cinnamon.

YIELD: *4 servings* EACH SERVING CONTAINS: *Carbohydrates:* 17 grams *Calories:* 105

russian apple kisel

Serve this chilled for a nice warm weather dessert; serve it warm in cooler weather.

4 cups peeled, cored, and quartered green apples
3 cups plus 1 tablespoon cold water
⅓ cup granulated sugar
1 tablespoon cornstarch

Place the apples and 3 cups of the cold water in a large pot over high heat. Bring to a boil, then reduce the heat and simmer, uncovered, for about 10 minutes, or until the apples are tender. Drain the apples, place them in a large bowl, and mash them. Stir in the sugar. Return the mixture to the pot and bring to a boil.

Place the cornstarch in a teacup and stir in the remaining tablespoon cold water to dissolve the cornstarch. Pour the cornstarch mixture into the fruit. Cook another 2 to 3 minutes, or until the mixture thickens. Spoon into individual serving dishes and refrigerate before serving.

YIELD: *4 servings* EACH SERVING CONTAINS: *Carbohydrates:* 31 grams *Calories:* 122

sweet-and-sour
strawberries

Surprisingly flavorful and so easy to make! Serve in fancy glasses for a special presentation.

2 cups fresh or frozen and thawed unsweetened strawberries
3 packets sugar substitute
2 tablespoons balsamic vinegar

Cut the strawberries in half and place them in a medium bowl. Sprinkle the strawberries with the sugar substitute and vinegar. Stir to combine. Serve chilled.

YIELD: *4 servings* EACH SERVING CONTAINS: *Carbohydrates:* 3 grams *Calories:* 24

cool strawberry fluff

A light, frothy dessert, this will melt in your mouth. Serve it after a heavy meal for the best effect.

1¼ cups sliced fresh or frozen and thawed unsweetened strawberries
2 envelopes unflavored gelatin
1 cup coarsely crushed ice

Place ½ cup of the strawberries in a blender and blend for about 5 seconds. Pour the strawberries into a small saucepan and heat over low heat and cook until their juice begins to boil, then transfer them back into the blender. Sprinkle the gelatin over the hot strawberries, cover, and blend for 30 seconds. Add the crushed ice and blend at low speed for 20 seconds. Place the remaining ¾ cup strawberries in a medium bowl, add the pureed strawberry mixture, and mix well. Pour into individual serving dishes or a serving bowl and chill before serving.

YIELD: *4 servings* EACH SERVING CONTAINS: *Carbohydrates:* 2 grams *Calories:* 26

english fresh strawberry pudding

Early English settlers found the strawberries in Virginia to be four times bigger than the ones they remembered from their homes in England. This is a traditional English recipe adapted for these wonderfully large strawberries.

> 2 cups fresh strawberries, hulled
> 2 tablespoons granulated sugar
> 2 packages (4-servings each) sugar-free strawberry gelatin mix
> 4 cups frozen lowfat non-dairy whipped topping, thawed

In a small bowl, crush the strawberries with a fork. Sprinkle the sugar over the strawberries. Mix, cover, and let stand for 1 hour. Drain the juice, reserving it in a measuring cup. Add enough water to make 1½ cups of liquid. Pour the liquid into a small saucepan over medium heat and bring to a boil. Stir in the gelatin. Remove from the heat and stir until the gelatin dissolves. Let cool, then pour the gelatin over the strawberries. Stir. Fold the whipped topping into the strawberry mixture. Transfer to a soufflé dish or other serving dish and refrigerate for several hours before serving. Serve chilled.

YIELD: *10 servings* EACH SERVING CONTAINS: *Carbohydrates:* 11 grams *Calories:* 72

fresh strawberry-melon medley

This is a favorite. I love the festive way it both looks and tastes. And you won't believe how simple it is to prepare!

1¼ cups frozen unsweetened sliced strawberries, thawed
1½ cups water
¼ cup cold water
½ teaspoon ground cinnamon
3 tablespoons cornstarch
3 packets sugar substitute
2 cups fresh strawberries, hulled and quartered
2 cups fresh or frozen honeydew melon balls

In a large saucepan over high heat, combine the thawed strawberries, 1½ cups water, and cinnamon. Bring to a boil, then lower the heat and simmer for 5 minutes. Pour into a blender or food processor and blend to puree. In another bowl, blend the cornstarch, ¼ cup cold water, and sugar substitute. Stir into the pureed strawberries. Return the mixture to the saucepan and bring to a boil over high heat, stirring constantly, then reduce the heat and simmer for 1 minute.

Pour the mixture into a large bowl and place a piece of wax paper or plastic wrap on the surface. Let cool slightly, then refrigerate to cool completely.

Before serving, remove the wax paper. Beat the puree with a whisk or electric mixer at medium speed until fluffy. Fold in the fresh strawberries and melon balls, reserving a few of each for garnish. Spoon into 6 parfait glasses and top with the reserved strawberries and melon balls.

YIELD: *6 servings* EACH SERVING CONTAINS: *Carbohydrates:* 20 grams *Calories:* 104

apple dessert

I love this recipe because it's fast and easy to make with ingredients that are usually on hand. Top with a little nutmeg and cinnamon if you like.

1 cup unsweetened applesauce
½ tablespoon fresh lemon juice
½ teaspoon vanilla extract
1 envelope unsweetened gelatin
¼ cup cold water
½ cup hot water

Mix together the applesauce, lemon juice, and vanilla in a large bowl. Place the gelatin in a small bowl with the cold water to soften for 5 minutes. Add the hot water and stir until the gelatin is dissolved. Stir into the applesauce mixture.

Cover and refrigerate for 1 hour until the mixture begins to stiffen. Remove from the refrigerator and beat with a whisk or electric mixer at medium speed until light.

YIELD: *6 servings* EACH SERVING CONTAINS: *Carbohydrates:* 5 grams *Calories:* 22

browned bananas

You can't imagine how satisfying a simple broiled banana can be until you've tried this recipe.

1 banana, peeled

Preheat the broiler. Coat a broiler pan with nonstick cooking spray. Slice the banana in half lengthwise. Place it on the broiler pan and place the pan under the broiler a few inches from the heat. Watch it carefully and remove from the oven when the banana becomes browned and bubbly. Serve hot. No garnish is necessary, but you might like to serve it with a small amount of frozen sugar-free nonfat vanilla yogurt.

YIELD: *2 servings* EACH SERVING CONTAINS: *Carbohydrates:* 15 grams *Calories:* 53

elegant blueberry dessert

A very fancy way to serve a simple berry dessert.

½ cup skim milk
2 teaspoons cornstarch
2 tablespoons orange liqueur (optional)
2 packets plus 1 teaspoon sugar substitute
2 teaspoons vanilla extract
1 large egg white
Pinch of cream of tartar
2 cups fresh or frozen and thawed unsweetened blueberries

Whisk together the milk, cornstarch, orange liqueur, if desired, and 2 packets sugar substitute in a medium saucepan, over medium heat making sure the cornstarch is dissolved. Bring to a boil, then reduce the heat and simmer, stirring constantly for a minute or two. Turn off the heat and stir in the vanilla and 1 teaspoon sugar substitute. Set aside to cool.

In a separate medium bowl, beat the egg white until it holds soft peaks, then add the cream of tartar and continue beating until stiff peaks form. Fold the egg white into the milk-cornstarch mixture, then stir in the blueberries. Pour into 4 fancy wine glasses and chill before serving.

YIELD: *4 servings* EACH SERVING CONTAINS: *Carbohydrates:* 12 grams *Calories:* 60

watermelon pudding

In the summer, there are always crowds of people (especially at meal times) at my house, but no matter what size watermelon, there's always some left over. This recipe puts it to good use.

3 cups pureed watermelon
1 tablespoon fresh lemon juice
1 envelope unflavored gelatin
1 package sugar-free strawberry gelatin mix
1½ cups nonfat cottage cheese

Coat 6 custard cups with nonstick cooking spray.

In a large saucepan, combine the pureed watermelon, lemon juice, and unflavored gelatin. Let stand for about 5 minutes to soften. Place over low heat and heat gently, stirring, until the gelatin dissolves. Remove from the heat and stir in the strawberry gelatin. Stir until the mixture is smooth and the gelatin is dissolved. Pour half the mixture into the custard cups. Place in the refrigerator and chill until set. Pour the remaining half of the mixture into a blender or food processor. Add the cottage cheese and blend. Pour the mixture into the custard cups and refrigerate until firm.

Serve in the custard cups or turn onto dessert plates. (To unmold the custard cups, run a warmed butter knife around the inside of each cup, then dip the cup into a pan of hot water for a few seconds. Place a plate over the top of the cup, invert, and shake onto the plate.)

YIELD: *6 servings* EACH SERVING CONTAINS: *Carbohydrates:* 15 grams *Calories:* 85

italian strawberries
and balsamic vinegar

T ry this recipe when strawberries are at their ripest.

2 cups hulled and halved strawberries
2 tablespoons balsamic vinegar

Place the strawberries in a medium bowl and carefully toss with the vinegar. Toss again just before serving.

YIELD: *4 servings* EACH SERVING CONTAINS: *Carbohydrates:* 6 grams *Calories:* 23

italian lemon water ice
(granita di limone)

I f you have an ice cream maker, you can use it for this recipe. If not, the ice cube technique I describe works fine.

⅓ cup granulated sugar
2½ cups water
1¼ cups fresh lemon juice

In a medium saucepan over high heat, combine the sugar and water. Bring to a boil and boil for 5 minutes. Remove from the heat and set aside to cool. Stir in the lemon juice.

Place in the bowl of an ice cream maker and freeze according to the manufacturer's directions. Alternatively, pour into ice cube trays and freeze. Pop out the cubes into a bowl and defrost slightly so that the ice is slushy prior to serving. Stir to combine.

YIELD: *6 servings* EACH SERVING CONTAINS: *Carbohydrates:* 16 grams *Calories:* 56

mexican fresh orange dessert

For maximum sweetness, be sure to take the time to pull off all of the pith from under the skin of the orange.

4 large sweet oranges, peeled, pith removed, and segmented
2 tablespoons grated orange peel
4 teaspoons finely chopped fresh mint
1 tablespoon powdered sugar
¼ cup light or flavored rum

Place alternate layers of orange segments sprinkled with orange peel, mint, powdered sugar, and rum in a glass or china bowl.

Cover with plastic wrap and refrigerate for several hours. Remove from the refrigerator, stir, and place in dessert glasses to serve.

YIELD: *6 servings* EACH SERVING CONTAINS: *Carbohydrates:* 15 grams *Calories:* 61

french flamed peaches

This is a truly impressive flaming dessert—the perfect way to end a meal!

4 ripe peaches, peeled and sliced
2 tablespoons fresh lemon juice
1 tablespoon unsalted butter
2 tablespoons granulated sugar
2 tablespoons brandy

Place the peach slices in a medium bowl and sprinkle with the lemon juice. Stir gently. Melt the butter in a flameproof serving dish. Add the sugar and the peaches. Stir over fairly high heat for just a few moments, but do not cook. Pour the brandy into a heatproof ladle, ignite with a match, and pour over the peaches. Serve immediately.

YIELD: *4 servings* EACH SERVING CONTAINS: *Carbohydrates:* 17 grams *Calories:* 107

mixed berry yogurt pudding

Many grocery stores sell mixed unsweetened frozen fruits. The combination of raspberries, strawberries, and blueberries is a natural for desserts. In season, use fresh berries.

1 (12-ounce) can evaporated nonfat milk
1 tablespoon cornstarch
3 packets plus 1 teaspoon sugar substitute
1 teaspoon almond extract
1 (12-ounce) bag frozen mixed unsweetened berries
2 cups plain or sugar-free vanilla nonfat yogurt

Combine the evaporated milk, cornstarch, and 3 packets sugar substitute together in a medium saucepan over medium heat. Heat just to boil, then reduce the heat and simmer stirring constantly with a wire whisk, for 5 minutes, or until the sauce thickens. Turn off the heat, then stir in the almond extract, 1 teaspoon sugar substitute, and the berries. Let cool and then fold in the yogurt.

YIELD: *8 servings* EACH SERVING CONTAINS: *Carbohydrates:* 12 grams *Calories:* 99

peaches and black cherries

This dramatic combination makes the most of succulent, fresh, ripe peaches and rich black cherries in season.

6 fresh peaches
1 tablespoon granulated sugar or 1 packet sugar substitute
⅓ cup water
12 fresh black cherries
¾ cup sugar-free fruit-flavored soda
   (black cherry or raspberry are good choices)

Bring a large pot of water to a boil. Using a large spoon, dip the peaches, one at a time, into the boiling water. Plunge the peaches into a bowl of cold water and slip off the skins. Discard the water.

Combine the sugar and water in a saucepan large enough to hold all six peaches and bring to boiling. Add the peaches and cook gently for 5 minutes, or just until softened. Cool the peaches in the liquid. Before serving, drain the peaches, reserving the liquid. Slice the peaches and divide them among 6 dessert glasses. Add 2 cherries to each glass. Combine the soda and peach juice and pour it over the fruit. Serve immediately or refrigerate until serving time.

YIELD: *6 servings* EACH SERVING CONTAINS: *Carbohydrates:* 10 grams *Calories:* 43

icy grapes

What could be easier? This is a wonderful sweet treat for low-carb dieters.

Wash the grapes and place them in a freezer bag. Place in the freezer for several hours or overnight. Serve in fancy wine glasses.

EACH ½ CUP GRAPES CONTAINS: *Carbohydrates:* 14 grams *Calories:* 54

puddings, custards, and gelatins

easy mixed fruit gelatin dessert

T he name says it all.

> 1 package (4 servings) sugar-free orange gelatin mix
> 1 cup boiling water
> 1 cup cold water
> ½ cup canned lite fruit chunks, drained
> Frozen lowfat non-dairy whipped topping, thawed (optional)

Place the gelatin in a large bowl. Stir in the boiling water and mix until the powder is dissolved. Stir in the cold water.

Arrange the fruit among 4 dessert dishes. Pour the gelatin mixture over the fruit. Cover and place in the refrigerator to chill for 3 to 4 hours. Top with a garnish of your favorite low-carb whipped topping, if desired.

YIELD: *4 servings* EACH SERVING CONTAINS: *Carbohydrates:* 5 grams *Calories:* 15

polish black bread pudding

Use your blender to make breadcrumbs from pumpernickel bread for this recipe. The more flavorful the bread, the better the pudding will be.

1 teaspoon white breadcrumbs
6 large eggs, separated
6 tablespoons granulated sugar
1 cup pumpernickel breadcrumbs
Ground cinnamon to taste
¼ teaspoon ground cloves
1 tablespoon unsalted butter or margarine, melted

Preheat the oven to 350°F. Butter a soufflé dish and line it with the white breadcrumbs.

In a large bowl, using an electric mixer, beat the egg whites until stiff. In another bowl, gently blend the egg yolks and sugar. Add the pumpernickel breadcrumbs, cinnamon, cloves, and melted butter. Mix thoroughly and fold in the beaten egg whites.

Pour the mixture into the soufflé dish and bake for 25 to 30 minutes, or until edges are dry and top springs back when pressed. Cool on a wire rack. Serve warm.

YIELD: *8 servings* EACH SERVING CONTAINS: *Carbohydrates:* 20 grams *Calories:* 160

german rye bread
and apple pudding

I make this using dark rye bread. The fabulous taste that comes from these simple ingredients never fails to impress.

11 slices pumpernickel, (dark) rye bread, cubed
1 cup unsweetened apple juice
1½ cups dry white wine
1½ pounds green apples, peeled, cored, and thickly sliced
5 tablespoons granulated sugar
½ teaspoon ground cinnamon
½ cup raisins
4 tablespoons unsalted butter or margarine, cut into small pieces

Preheat the oven to 400°F. Grease a 1-quart casserole well.

Place two-thirds of the bread cubes in a large bowl and pour the apple juice and wine over them. Stir. Place a thick layer of the mixture on the bottom of the casserole. Add a layer of apples, then sprinkle with some of the sugar and cinnamon. Continue layering until the apples are used up, finishing with sugar and cinnamon. Sprinkle the raisins on top followed by the remaining bread. Dot the top with the butter.

Bake for 45 minutes, or until top is crusty. Serve warm.

YIELD: *10 servings* EACH SERVING CONTAINS: *Carbohydrates:* 35 grams *Calories:* 215

orange cottage cheese dessert

My mother loves this not-too-sweet dessert. I make it in the morning before work and refrigerate it while I'm away.

1 package (4 servings) sugar-free orange gelatin mix
1 cup boiling water
1 cup cold water
1 cup fat-free small curd cottage cheese
2 cups diced orange sections

Place the gelatin in a large bowl. Add the boiling water and stir until the gelatin is dissolved. Stir in the cold water. Place the mixture in a food processor or blender and add the cottage cheese. Blend until the mixture is smooth.

Divide the mixture among 4 dessert dishes. Cover and place in the refrigerator to chill for 3 to 4 hours before serving. Garnish with the oranges just before serving.

YIELD: *4 servings* EACH SERVING CONTAINS: *Carbohydrates:* 16 grams *Calories:* 79

creamy melon gelatin dessert

This recipe makes great use of leftover cantaloupe or melon.

1 package (4 servings) sugar-free lime gelatin mix
1 cup boiling water
½ cup sugar-free lowfat vanilla ice cream
½ cup cold water
½ cup fresh or frozen cantaloupe or honeydew melon pieces

Place the gelatin in a large bowl. Add the boiling water and stir until the gelatin is dissolved. Stir in the ice cream and cold water.

Arrange the melon pieces among 4 dessert dishes. Pour the gelatin mixture over the fruit. Cover and place in the refrigerator to chill for 3 to 4 hours before serving.

YIELD: *4 servings* EACH SERVING CONTAINS: *Carbohydrates:* 7 grams *Calories:* 23

scandinavian pudding

T his is a variation of *klappgröt,* a traditional Scandinavian dessert.

6 ounces frozen apple juice concentrate
2½ cups water
4 tablespoons farina
½ cup unsweetened pineapple juice (from a can of crushed pineapple)

Combine the apple juice concentrate and water in a large saucepan over high heat. Bring to a rapid boil. Gradually add the farina, stirring. Reduce the heat to low and cook gently for 5 minutes, or until thickened. Remove from the heat and transfer to a medium bowl. Beat by hand or with an electric mixer until the mixture is smooth. Stir in the pineapple juice. Pour into 6 individual pudding dishes, cover, and place in the refrigerator to chill before serving.

YIELD: *6 servings* EACH SERVING CONTAINS: *Carbohydrates:* 18 grams *Calories:* 88

irish tipsy parson

The name says it all! Make this in the morning and you'll have an impressive dessert ready to serve after dinner. The first time I made this the taste-testers devoured it in minutes.

1 cup whole fresh or frozen and thawed unsweetened strawberries
1 tablespoon granulated sugar
½ angel food cake, cubed
3 tablespoons sweet sherry
1 package (4 servings) sugar-free vanilla pudding mix (not instant)
2 cups 1% lowfat milk
1 teaspoon vanilla extract
1 cup frozen lowfat non-dairy whipped topping,
    plus more for serving (optional)
¼ cup toasted almonds, for serving (optional)

Combine the strawberries and sugar in a small bowl and set aside. Toss the cake cubes and sherry together in a medium bowl and set aside. Make the vanilla pudding according to the package directions using the lowfat milk. Stir in the vanilla. Cool for 15 minutes. Stir in the whipped topping.

Place alternate layers of the cake cubes, strawberries, and pudding in a serving bowl or individual dishes. Cover and refrigerate for at least 4 hours before serving. Decorate with whipped topping and toasted almonds, if desired.

YIELD: *10 servings* EACH SERVING CONTAINS: *Carbohydrates:* 25 grams *Calories:* 128

madigan's velvet trousers

A light and lovely Irish gelatin dessert. You may have trouble getting it to the table—at my house spoon marks start appearing in the surface the minute it hits the refrigerator.

1 envelope unflavored gelatin
¼ cup cold water
1½ tablespoons honey (light colored is best)
2 tablespoons Irish Mist liqueur
2 cups frozen lowfat non-dairy whipped topping, thawed

Pour the gelatin into the top of a double boiler over simmering water. Add the water and stir until the gelatin dissolves. Remove from over the simmering water and slowly mix in the honey and Irish Mist. Cook, then gently fold in the whipped topping using a rubber scraper.

Spoon into 4 small glasses or dessert goblets. Tightly cover the glasses with aluminum foil or plastic wrap and refrigerate for several hours before serving.

YIELD: *4 servings* EACH SERVING CONTAINS: *Carbohydrates:* 12 grams *Calories:* 116

hawaiian custard

T his is another one of my grandmother's recipes updated with sugar
substitute to make it low carb but equally sweet and creamy.

2 cups skim milk
6 packets sugar substitute
⅓ cup pearl tapioca
¼ cup eggs or egg substitute
1 tablespoon cold water
1 cup drained unsweetened canned crushed pineapple

Place the milk in the top of a double boiler over simmering water. Add the
sugar substitute and tapioca and cook over boiling water until thickened, stirring occasionally. (If you do not have a double boiler, stir constantly to avoid
burning the milk.) With an electric mixer, beat in the egg followed by the cold
water. Pour the hot liquid tapioca over the egg mixture, then return to the top
of the double boiler and cook 3 to 5 minutes, stirring constantly. When the
mixture is smooth and thick, beat in the crushed pineapple. Divide the custard
among 8 dessert cups, cover, and refrigerate to chill thoroughly before serving.

YIELD: *8 servings* EACH SERVING CONTAINS: *Carbohydrates:* 15 grams *Calories:* 62

thanksgiving custard

This fall pudding is so low in calories, fat, and carbs that it's easy to fit in with any meal.

1 (15-ounce) can pumpkin puree
2 teaspoons pumpkin pie spice
2 teaspoons olive oil
1 tablespoon fructose
2 teaspoons vanilla extract
7 packets sugar substitute
1 cup skim milk
4 large egg whites

Preheat the oven to 375°F. Coat 10 custard cups with nonstick cooking spray.

Place the pumpkin, pumpkin pie spice, oil, fructose, vanilla, and sugar substitute in a large bowl. Use a wire whisk to mix completely.

In a large saucepan, heat the milk over medium heat just to the boiling point. Whisk the milk into the pumpkin mixture. In a separate bowl, use an electric mixer to beat the egg whites until stiff. Fold the egg whites into the pumpkin mixture, making sure it is well mixed.

Pour the mixture into the custard cups and place them in 1 very large or 2 medium ovenproof pans. Carefully pour boiling water into the baking pans, taking care that water doesn't spill into the filled cups.

Bake for 35 minutes, or until a knife inserted into the center of a custard cup comes out clean. Remove from the oven and place on racks to cool. Cover and place in the refrigerator to chill before serving.

YIELD: *10 servings* EACH SERVING CONTAINS: *Carbohydrates:* 7 grams *Calories:* 43

pineapple mousse

This was a great success when I served it to my mother and her friends—they had no idea it was low carb!

1 (20-ounce) can crushed pineapple packed in juice, drained
2 tablespoons fructose
1 cup evaporated skim milk, chilled
1 tablespoon fresh lemon juice
1 envelope unflavored gelatin

Place the pineapple and fructose in a blender or food processor and puree. Set aside. In a large bowl, whip the evaporated milk until thick and creamy. Place the lemon juice in the top of a double boiler over simmering water and sprinkle the gelatin over the lemon juice. Let stand for 3 to 5 minutes, then stir until dissolved. Stir the gelatin into the whipped milk, then fold in the pineapple mixture. Spoon into a large dessert dish. Cover and place in the refrigerator to chill until set before serving.

YIELD: *16 servings* EACH SERVING CONTAINS: *Carbohydrates:* 15 grams *Calories:* 51

black cherry gelatin

Y ou can use any flavor sugar-free soda here, even ginger ale, for a much more subtle flavor than what you'll get with packaged gelatin from the supermarket.

¼ cup cold water
1 envelope unflavored gelatin
2 packets sugar substitute
2 cups sugar-free black cherry soda
Fresh fruit slices, for serving (optional)

Place the water in the top of a double boiler over simmering water. Sprinkle the gelatin on top and let stand for 5 minutes, then stir the gelatin until dissolved. In a medium bowl, combine the sugar substitute and soda. Pour the gelatin into the soda mixture. Cover and place in the refrigerator to chill until set, about 3 hours. Garnish with fresh fruit slices, if desired.

YIELD: *4 servings* EACH SERVING CONTAINS: *Carbohydrates:* less than 1 gram *Calories:* 7

swedish citrus fromage

This is so fast and easy to whip up and it works especially well after a seafood meal.

2 teaspoons unflavored gelatin
2 tablespoons cold water
2 tablespoons fresh orange juice
1 tablespoon fresh lemon juice
1 teaspoon grated orange peel
4 large eggs, separated
2 tablespoons granulated sugar (optional)
3 packets sugar substitute

Combine the gelatin and water in a small saucepan. Let stand for 5 minutes, then place over low heat, stirring, until the gelatin dissolves. Set aside to cool. Stir in the orange juice, lemon juice, and orange peel.

Beat the egg yolks and sugar, if desired, in a medium bowl together until thick and light. Beat in the gelatin mixture and the sugar substitute. In a separate bowl, beat the egg whites until stiff peaks form. Use a rubber spatula to gently fold the egg whites into the gelatin mixture. The mixture should be evenly yellow.

Spoon into 6 dessert dishes. Cover and place in the refrigerator to chill until set, about 3 hours.

YIELD: *6 servings* EACH SERVING CONTAINS: *Carbohydrates:* less than 1 gram *Calories:* 58

ricotta cheese pudding

A rich and very special European-style pudding for grown-ups.

1 pound fat-free ricotta cheese
2 tablespoons frozen lowfat non-dairy whipped topping, thawed
2 tablespoons Triple Sec
1 teaspoon sugar substitute
2 ounces low-carb chocolate bar, coarsely chopped
¼ cup Not-Too-Sweet Chocolate Sauce (page 30)

Place the ricotta in a blender or food processor and blend until smooth. Add the whipped topping, Triple Sec, and sugar substitute and blend again until smooth. Transfer to a large bowl and fold in the chocolate.

Cover the bowl and refrigerate for 1 hour before serving. Serve topped with Not-Too-Sweet Chocolate Sauce.

YIELD: *4 servings* EACH SERVING CONTAINS: *Carbohydrates:* 16 grams *Calories:* 139

mocha pudding

For a sharper coffee taste, you can use instant espresso powder.

1 package (4 servings) sugar-free chocolate pudding mix
1½ cups skim milk
3 teaspoons instant coffee powder

Combine all the ingredients in a small saucepan over medium heat. Bring to a boil and cook, stirring constantly, until the pudding has thickened, about 5 minutes. Transfer to a bowl, cover, and refrigerate for 1 hour before serving.

YIELD: *4 servings* EACH SERVING CONTAINS: *Carbohydrates:* 6 grams *Calories:* 36

chocolate mousse pudding

Light and luscious, and will meet a chocoholic's needs.

1½ cups skim milk
1 package (4 servings) sugar-free, fat-free, instant chocolate
    pudding mix
1 cup frozen lowfat, non-dairy whipped topping, slightly softened
1 tablespoon chocolate liqueur or crème de cacao

Pour the milk into a large bowl. Add the pudding mix and beat according to the package directions. Add the whipped topping and liqueur. Stir gently until just blended. Spoon into 5 dessert dishes.

YIELD: *5 servings* EACH SERVING CONTAINS: *Carbohydrates:* 4 grams *Calories:* 37

quick microwave custard

When you make this you won't believe how quick making custard can be.

1½ cups skim milk
3 large eggs or equivalent egg substitute
2 tablespoons granulated sugar
3 packages sugar substitute
1 teaspoon vanilla extract
¼ teaspoon ground nutmeg

Pour the milk into a glass measuring cup and microwave on high for 3 minutes. In a large bowl, whisk together the eggs, sugar, sugar substitute, and vanilla. Gradually stir in the hot milk.

Pour into a 1 quart glass baking dish and sprinkle nutmeg on top. Microwave on defrost for 10 minutes. The custard will become firmer as it sets. Transfer to a bowl, cover, and refrigerate for at least 1 hour before serving.

YIELD: *4 servings* EACH SERVING CONTAINS: *Carbohydrates:* 12 grams *Calories:* 117

raspberry cream gelatin

The sour cream here gives a mousse-like effect. For a special look, save a few raspberries and add a few mint leaves to garnish.

> 1 package (4 servings) sugar-free raspberry gelatin mix
> 1 cup boiling water
> ½ cup fat-free sour cream
> ½ cup cold water
> ½ cup frozen unsweetened raspberries, thawed

Place the gelatin in a large bowl. Add the boiling water and stir until the gelatin is dissolved. Stir in the sour cream and cold water.

Arrange the raspberries in 4 dessert bowls. Pour the gelatin mixture over the raspberries. Cover and place in the refrigerator to chill until set, 3 to 4 hours.

YIELD: *4 servings* EACH SERVING CONTAINS: *Carbohydrates:* 7 grams *Calories:* 31

strawberry yogurt dessert

The yogurt gives this pudding its creamy texture. It's a great snack too.

1 package (4 servings) sugar-free strawberry gelatin mix
¾ cup boiling water
½ cup cold water
Ice cubes
1 cup plain or sugar-free vanilla fat-free yogurt
½ cup hulled and sliced fresh strawberries, plus more for garnish (optional)
4 mint leaves, for garnish (optional)

Place the gelatin in a large bowl. Add the boiling water and stir until the gelatin is dissolved. Pour the cold water into a 2-cup measure. Add enough ice cubes to reach the 1¼ cup mark, then pour into a food processor. Add the gelatin mixture and process until most of the ice disappears.

Place the strawberries in a serving bowl. Put the yogurt and gelatin mixture over the fruit. Cover and refrigerate to chill for 1 to 2 hours. Top with your favorite whipped topping and garnish with strawberry slices and mint leaves, if desired.

YIELD: *4 servings* EACH SERVING CONTAINS: *Carbohydrates:* 8 grams *Calories:* 40

ginger-strawberry cooler

Ginger is a flavor favored by people who live in tropical climates because of its cooling properties. Try making this easy cooler for the hottest days of summer.

> 1 package (4 servings) sugar-free strawberry-kiwi gelatin mix
> 1 cup boiling water
> ¼ teaspoon ground ginger
> 1 cup sugar-free ginger ale
> ½ cup sliced fresh or frozen and thawed unsweetened strawberries
> Frozen lowfat non-dairy whipped topping, thawed, for serving

Place the gelatin in a large bowl. Add the boiling water and ginger and stir until the gelatin is dissolved. Stir in the ginger ale.

Arrange the strawberries in 4 dessert bowls. Pour the gelatin mixture over the strawberries. Cover and place in the refrigerator to chill for 3 to 4 hours before serving. Top with your favorite whipped topping, if desired.

YIELD: *4 servings* EACH SERVING CONTAINS: *Carbohydrates:* 3 grams *Calories:* 10

strawberry layered dessert

Y ou can also make this recipe with sugar-free fat-free frozen yogurt.

1 package (4 servings) sugar-free strawberry-banana gelatin mix
¾ cup boiling water
½ cup cold water
Ice cubes
½ cup sugar-free lowfat vanilla ice cream
½ cup fresh hulled and sliced strawberries
Frozen lowfat non-dairy whipped topping, thawed, for serving

Place the gelatin in a large bowl. Add the boiling water and stir until the gelatin is dissolved. Pour the cold water into a 2-cup measure. Add enough ice cubes to reach the 1¼ cup mark, then pour into a food processor. Add the gelatin mixture and process until most of the ice disappears.

Divide the gelatin mixture between 2 bowls. Add the ice cream to one bowl and the strawberries to the other. Mix until smooth. Spoon a layer of the fruit mixture in each of 4 individual dessert dishes, followed by an ice cream layer. Cover and refrigerate to chill until set, about 1 hour, before serving. Top with your favorite whipped topping.

YIELD: *4 servings* EACH SERVING CONTAINS: *Carbohydrates:* 6 grams *Calories:* 22

strawberry-banana cubes

For a special effect use cookie cutters to carve out fun shapes—kids will love it.

1 package (4 servings) sugar-free strawberry-banana gelatin mix
¾ cup boiling water
¾ cup cold water
1 medium banana, sliced
½ cup sliced fresh strawberries (optional)

Place the gelatin in a large bowl. Add the boiling water and stir until the powder is dissolved. Stir in the cold water.

Arrange the fruit in an 8-by-8-inch baking pan. Pour the gelatin over the fruit. Cover and refrigerate to chill for 3 to 4 hours, until the mixture sets. To serve, cut into cubes and arrange the cubes in a circle around the edge of a plate. If you like, you can garnish with a small piece of fresh fruit or a dollop of your favorite whipped topping.

YIELD: *4 servings* EACH SERVING CONTAINS: *Carbohydrates:* 10 grams *Calories:* 36

german bavarian cream

Smooth and luscious, this will melt in your mouth.

1 envelope unflavored gelatin
¼ cup 1% lowfat milk, chilled
4 large egg yolks or equivalent egg substitute
¼ cup granulated sugar
1 cup 1% lowfat milk
1 teaspoon vanilla extract
1 cup frozen lowfat non-dairy whipped topping, thawed

Place the gelatin in a cup and stir in the ¼ cup cold milk. Set aside. Place the egg yolks in a large bowl and beat until thickened. Gradually beat in the sugar. In the top of a double boiler over simmering water or in a heavy saucepan, heat the 1 cup milk until scalding. Set aside to cool. Gradually add the egg mixture and cook, stirring constantly, until thick enough to coat a spoon. Remove from the heat. Whisk in the vanilla and gelatin, until smooth.

Refrigerate for about 30 minutes, or until thoroughly cooled. Fold in the whipped topping. Cover and refrigerate for another 2 hours, until firm, before serving.

YIELD: *6 servings* EACH SERVING CONTAINS: *Carbohydrates:* 15 grams *Calories:* 122

pear and banana gelatin dessert

I f you like your fruit floating in gelatin rather than at the bottom, let the gelatin set for 20 to 30 minutes and then stir in the fruit and nuts.

> 1 package (4 servings) sugar-free strawberry-banana gelatin mix
> 1 cup boiling water
> ½ teaspoon rum-flavored extract
> 1 cup cold water
> ½ cup sliced fresh or canned "lite" pears, drained
> ½ cup sliced bananas
> 2 tablespoons finely chopped walnuts (optional)
> Frozen lowfat non-dairy whipped topping, thawed (optional)

Place the gelatin in a large bowl. Add the boiling water and rum-flavored extract and stir until the gelatin is dissolved. Stir in the cold water.

Arrange the fruit and walnuts, if desired, in 4 individual dessert bowls. Pour the gelatin mixture over the fruit. Cover and refrigerate to chill until firm, 3 to 4 hours, before serving. Top with your favorite whipped topping, if desired.

YIELD: *4 servings* EACH SERVING CONTAINS: *Carbohydrates:* 12 grams *Calories:* 43

lime and banana gelatin dessert

As in the previous recipe, if you'd like the bananas to float, wait to add them until after the gelatin has started to set.

1 package (4 servings) sugar-free lime gelatin mix
1 cup boiling water
½ cup cold water
½ cup fat-free sour cream
1 medium banana, sliced

Place the gelatin in a large bowl. Add the boiling water and stir until the gelatin is dissolved. Add the cold water and sour cream and stir until the sour cream is completely blended.

Arrange the banana slices in 4 dessert dishes. Pour the gelatin mixture over the bananas. Cover and refrigerate to chill until firm, 3 to 4 hours, before serving.

YIELD: *4 servings* EACH SERVING CONTAINS: *Carbohydrates:* 12 grams *Calories:* 50

key lime pudding

You'll find this light and tart pudding very refreshing.

   1 package (4 servings) sugar-free lime gelatin mix
   ¾ cup boiling water
   1 tablespoon Key lime juice
   ½ cup cold water
   Ice cubes
   1¾ cups frozen lowfat non-dairy whipped topping, thawed

Place the gelatin in a large bowl. Add the boiling water and stir until the gelatin is dissolved. Stir in the lime juice. Pour the cold water into a 2-cup measuring cup. Add enough ice cubes to reach the 1¼ cup mark, then pour into a blender or food processor. Add the gelatin mixture and blend until most of the ice disappears. Add the whipped topping and blend again to mix.

Pour into 8 individual serving bowls. Cover and refrigerate to chill until set, about 1 hour, before serving.

YIELD: *8 servings* EACH SERVING CONTAINS: *Carbohydrates:* 5 grams *Calories:* 37

lemon pudding

A nice variation on Key Lime Pudding. For a big crowd, make one recipe of each.

Prepare Key Lime Pudding, but substitute sugar-free lemon gelatin mix for the lime gelatin mix and lemon juice for the Key lime juice.

YIELD: *8 servings* EACH SERVING CONTAINS: *Carbohydrates:* 5 grams *Calories:* 37

soufflés
and crêpes

salzburg soufflé

A classic Austrian-style soufflé with a fresh lemon tang.

3 large egg yolks
1 teaspoon vanilla extract
Grated peel of ½ lemon
2 tablespoons all-purpose flour
5 large egg whites
Pinch of salt
2 tablespoons confectioners' sugar

Preheat the oven to 350°F. Grease an 8½-inch soufflé dish.

In a large bowl, beat the egg yolks with the vanilla, lemon peel, and flour. In a separate bowl, whip the egg whites with the salt until stiff peaks begin to form. Gradually beat in the confectioners' sugar and beat until stiff peaks form. Gently fold the egg whites into the egg yolk mixture.

Spoon into the soufflé dish. With a spatula, form into 3 separate mounds. Bake for 15 to 20 minutes, or until lightly browned on top. As with all soufflés, serve immediately.

YIELD: *6 servings* EACH SERVING CONTAINS: *Carbohydrates:* 5 grams *Calories:* 64

french strawberry and peach soufflé

T his soufflé is foolproof, but it still needs to be served right away.

2 large ripe peaches, diced
1⅔ cups (13 ounces) frozen and thawed unsweetened strawberries,
   diced
⅓ cup Grand Marnier
4 large egg yolks, separated
2 tablespoons confectioners' sugar
Pinch of salt

Preheat the oven to 400°F. Grease 4 individual soufflé dishes well.

Combine the peaches, strawberries, and Grand Marnier in a medium bowl and marinate for 2 to 3 hours. In a large bowl, cream the egg yolks and confectioners' sugar until pale and creamy. Spoon the marinated fruit and its liquid into the egg yolk mixture.

In another large bowl, beat the egg whites with the salt until stiff peaks form. Gently fold the egg whites into the egg yolk mixture.

Turn into the soufflé dishes. Bake for about 15 minutes, or until the soufflés have risen and are golden brown on top. Serve immediately.

YIELD: *4 servings* EACH SERVING CONTAINS: *Carbohydrates:* 23 grams *Calories:* 210

cherry cheese suzette

Rich and sweet—a brunch favorite.

BATTER
¼ cup unsalted butter or margarine, softened
2 large eggs or equivalent egg substitute
1¼ cups all-purpose flour
1 teaspoon baking powder
¾ cup skim milk

FILLING
2 cups fat-free cottage cheese
1 teaspoon butter-flavored extract
1 package sugar substitute
½ cup all-fruit cherry preserves

Preheat the oven to 350°F. Coat an 8-inch square baking pan with nonstick cooking spray.

Place the butter in the bowl of an electric mixer. Add the eggs and beat at medium speed until smooth. In a medium bowl, combine the flour and baking powder. With the mixer running at low speed, alternately add the flour mixture and the milk to the egg mixture. Mix for 2 minutes. Spoon half of the batter into the prepared pan.

To make the filling, combine the cottage cheese, butter-flavored extract, and sugar substitute in a medium bowl and evenly spread over the batter. Dot with the cherry preserves. Carefully pour the remaining batter on top. Bake for 50 to 60 minutes, or until the top is lightly browned. Serve hot.

YIELD: *9 servings* **EACH SERVING CONTAINS:** *Carbohydrates:* 29 grams *Calories:* 164

hot apple soufflé

Your house will smell wonderful while this soufflé is in the oven.

½ cup margarine or unsalted butter
½ cup all-purpose flour
2 cups skim milk
2 tablespoons granulated sugar
1 package sugar substitute
Grated peel from ½ lemon
2 medium apples
4 large eggs, separated
2 tablespoons slivered toasted almonds

Melt the margarine in a medium saucepan over medium heat. Stir in the flour, then the milk. Cook, stirring constantly, until smooth and thickened, about 5 minutes. Remove from the heat and stir in the sugar, sugar substitute, and lemon peel. Let cool slightly, stirring occasionally.

Meanwhile, core the apples and cut each into about 10 wedges. Arrange the apple wedges evenly over the bottom of a casserole that measures 8 cups to the brim and has been sprayed with a cooking spray. Beat the egg whites in a large bowl until stiff. Whisk the yolks into the flour-milk mixture, then carefully fold in the egg whites. Spoon over the apples, then sprinkle the almonds on top. Bake for 1¼ hours, or until lightly browned and firm. Serve immediately.

YIELD: *8 servings* EACH SERVING CONTAINS: *Carbohydrates:* 15 grams *Calories:* 229

chocolate soufflé

T his one is absolutely wonderful.

½ cup unsweetened cocoa powder
2 tablespoons powdered sugar
½ cup measures-like-sugar sugar substitute
7 packets sugar substitute
2 tablespoons cornstarch
Dash of salt (optional)
½ cup skim milk
½ cup water
4 large egg whites
½ teaspoon cream of tartar
1 large egg or a ¼ cup egg substitute
1 teaspoon vanilla extract
Confectioners' sugar, for dusting

Preheat the oven to 400°F. Coat a 6-cup soufflé dish with nonstick cooking spray.

Sift the cocoa, powdered sugar, measures-like-sugar, sugar substitute, cornstarch, and salt, if desired, together twice into the top of a double boiler placed over boiling water. Add the milk and water and whisk constantly until the mixture is smooth and thick, about 8 minutes.

Remove from the heat. In a separate bowl, beat the egg whites with an electric mixer until they hold their shape. Add the cream of tartar and continue beating until stiff peaks form. Stir the eggs and vanilla into the chocolate mixture. Add a small amount of the beaten egg whites into the chocolate mixture to lighten. Then use a rubber spatula to fold in the rest of the egg whites.

Pour the mixture into the prepared soufflé dish and bake for 20 minutes, or until the center is still a little runny when the soufflé is removed from the oven. Do not overcook. Immediately, dust with confectioners' sugar, and serve.

YIELD: *8 servings* EACH SERVING CONTAINS: *Carbohydrates: 8 grams Calories: 54*

berry soufflé

T his lovely and impressive soufflé tastes as good as it looks.

1¾ cups mixed fresh or frozen and thawed unsweetened red berries
1 tablespoon Chambord or fruit-flavored liqueur
5 large egg whites

Preheat the oven to 350°F. Coat a 2-quart soufflé dish with nonstick cooking spray.

Place the berries and Chambord in a blender or food processor and puree. In a large bowl, beat the egg whites until stiff but not dry. Fold the berry puree into the egg whites.

Spoon the mixture into the prepared soufflé dish, place the soufflé dish on a baking sheet, and bake for 30 to 35 minutes, or until it has risen and top has browned. Serve immediately.

YIELD: *6 servings* EACH SERVING CONTAINS: *Carbohydrates:* 6 grams *Calories:* 31

lemon sponge soufflé

This is an adaptation of one of my grandmother Lily's favorites.
It's a light touch after a heavy meal, and an especially wonderful
dessert after a fish meal.

1 tablespoon all-purpose flour
2 tablespoons granulated sugar
3 packages sugar substitute
2 tablespoons fresh lemon juice
1½ teaspoons grated lemon peel
2 large eggs, separated
1 cup skim milk

Preheat the oven to 350°F. Coat a casserole or 1-quart soufflé pan with nonstick
cooking spray.

Combine the flour, sugar, sugar substitute, lemon juice, and lemon peel in a
large bowl. In a separate bowl, use an electric mixer at high speed to beat the
egg yolks until lemon colored. Add the egg yolks to the flour mixture and blend
well. In another bowl, beat the egg whites until stiff. Fold the egg whites into
the egg yolk mixture.

Spoon the mixture into the prepared casserole and place the casserole in a large
baking pan. Fill the pan with hot water to come halfway up the sides of the
casserole. Bake for 35 to 40 minutes, or until the top is lightly browned. Serve
immediately.

YIELD: *4 servings* EACH SERVING CONTAINS: *Carbohydrates:* 12 grams *Calories:* 95

sweet crêpe batter

I f the first crêpe doesn't move easily in the pan, thin the batter with a little additional milk.

2 large eggs or equivalent egg substitute
3 tablespoons canola oil
1 teaspoon butter-flavored extract
1 cup skim milk
2 tablespoons fruit-flavored liqueur
½ cup all-purpose flour
1 tablespoon granulated sugar
Butter-flavored cooking spray

Place the ingredients in a blender or food processor in the order listed. Blend at high speed for a minute or more, until the batter is well blended. Cover and refrigerate for at least an hour. To prepare the crêpes, coat a medium heavy-bottomed frying pan with butter-flavored cooking spray. Place over medium heat until the pan is hot. Remove the pan from the heat and pour ¼ cup of the batter into the center of the pan. Tilt the pan quickly in all directions to coat the bottom. Return the pan to the heat and cook for about 1 minute. Shake the pan to loosen the crêpe. Lift one edge of the crepe—if it's a light golden color, the first side is done. Flip the crêpe with a spatula and cook for about 30 seconds, or until set. This side probably won't look as good, so it should become the inside when you fill the crêpes. Repeat with the rest of the batter, coating the pan with additional butter-flavored extract as needed.

YIELD: *6 crêpes* EACH SERVING CONTAINS: *Carbohydrates:* 6 grams *Calories:* 80

blintz filling

T he butter-flavored extract gives this filling its rich flavor.

1 pound fat-free cottage cheese
2 packages sugar substitute
1 teaspoon butter-flavored extract
2 tablespoons frozen lowfat non-dairy whipped topping, thawed

Place all the ingredients in a blender or food processor and blend until smooth. To fill the crêpes, place a spoonful of the mixture on the back of each crêpe and roll them up.

YIELD: *Filling for 6 crêpes* EACH SERVING CONTAINS: *Carbohydrates:* 5 grams *Calories:* 49

austrian raspberry cream crêpes

You'll think you're in Vienna as you eat these.

1 recipe Sweet Crêpe Batter (page 135)
1 cup all-fruit seedless raspberry preserves
½ cup water
2 tablespoons raspberry-flavored brandy (optional)
1½ cups fat-free sour cream
¾ cup finely chopped toasted almonds (optional)

Prepare the crêpes according to the directions on page 135, placing wax paper between each crêpe as you stack them and a kitchen towel over the top to keep them warm. In a small saucepan over medium heat, combine the preserves, water, and brandy, if desired. Cook for about 5 minutes, stirring constantly, until combined. Remove from heat.

In a small bowl, combine the sour cream and almonds, if desired.

Spread 2 tablespoons of the raspberry mixture on the back of each crêpe, and roll them up. Arrange the crêpes on dessert plates, seam side down. Spoon on a dollop of sour cream and garnish with any remaining raspberry mixture.

YIELD: *12 servings* EACH SERVING CONTAINS: *Carbohydrates:* 21 grams *Calories:* 148

kaiser schmarren

Ｔhis is an old German recipe.

1 recipe Sweet Crêpe Batter (page 135)
½ cup orange juice
1 teaspoon orange extract
½ cup golden raisins
1 teaspoon unsalted butter or margarine
½ cup sliced almonds

Prepare the crêpes according to the directions on page 135, placing wax paper between each crêpe as you stack them and a kitchen towel over the top to keep them warm. In a small bowl, combine the orange juice, orange extract, and raisins. Let stand for about 30 minutes, until the raisins are plump. Melt the butter in a small frying pan over medium heat. Add the almonds and toast until golden, stirring constantly. Add the almonds to the raisin mixture.

Spread 1 heaping tablespoon of the raisin mixture on the back of each crêpe, and roll them up. Arrange the crêpes on dessert plates, seam side down.

YIELD: *12 servings* EACH SERVING CONTAINS: *Carbohydrates:* 8 grams *Calories:* 68

crêpes marcelles

Roll these crêpes just before serving. In a pinch you can use instant pudding in place of the tart filling.

1 recipe Sweet Crêpe Batter (page 135)
1 recipe Vanilla Tart Filling (page 38)
1 tablespoon cognac
1 teaspoon orange extract
¼ cup unsweetened crushed pineapple in juice, drained

Prepare the crêpes according to the directions on page 135, placing wax paper between each crêpe as you stack them and a kitchen towel over the top to keep them warm.

Prepare the Vanilla Tart Filling and add the cognac, orange extract, and crushed pineapple.

Spoon the filling on the back of each crêpe and roll them. Arrange the crêpes on dessert plates, seam side down.

YIELD: *12 servings* EACH SERVING CONTAINS: *Carbohydrates:* 7 grams *Calories:* 64

russian dessert pancakes

These are a staple in Moscow restaurants, and are a great comfort food. The batter can be made the day before and the pancakes can be made before you serve dinner.

1 cup all-purpose flour
2 cups 1% lowfat milk
2 large eggs, separated
2 tablespoons granulated sugar
¼ teaspoon salt
2 tablespoons unsalted butter or margarine
½ cup all-fruit blueberry (or other berry) jam, for garnish

Place the flour in a large bowl and beat in the milk ½ cup at a time. Then beat in the egg yolks, sugar, salt, and butter to thoroughly combine. Set the batter aside in a cool but not cold place for at least 3 hours.

Just before making the pancakes, beat the egg whites in a large bowl until stiff peaks form. Use a rubber spatula to fold the egg whites into the batter.

Preheat the oven to 250°F. Lightly coat a 5- to 6-inch crêpe pan or skillet with a nonstick cooking spray and place it over medium heat to warm. Pour in ½ cup of the batter, tilting the pan to spread evenly. Cook for about 3 minutes, or until golden. Flip the pancake and cook on the other side until golden. Slide the pancake onto an ovenproof platter and keep warm in the oven while you cook the remaining pancakes, placing each in the oven as they come out of the pan. Serve on heated dessert plates and garnish with berry jam.

YIELD: *10 pancakes* EACH SERVING CONTAINS: *Carbohydrates:* 24 grams *Calories:* 151

french baked cherry pancakes

Whenever mountains of fresh cherries appear in the market, I think of this recipe. I think you'll love it as much as I do.

1½ pounds black cherries, pitted
4 large eggs, lightly beaten, or equivalent egg substitute
Pinch of salt
¼ cup granulated sugar
½ cup all-purpose flour
4 tablespoons unsalted butter or margarine
1 cup 1% lowfat milk
Frozen lowfat non-dairy whipped topping, thawed, for serving
   (optional)

Preheat the oven to 400°F. Grease a wide and shallow ovenproof dish well and arrange the cherries over the dish.

In a large bowl combine the eggs, salt, and sugar. Add the flour and beat well. Melt 2 tablespoons of the butter and beat it into the batter, then beat in the milk. Pour the mixture over the cherries. Dot with the remaining 2 tablespoons butter.

Bake for 35 to 40 minutes, or until set. Serve either hot or cold, topped with whipped topping, if desired.

YIELD: *12 servings* EACH SERVING CONTAINS: *Carbohydrates:* 16 grams *Calories:* 128

irish shrove tuesday pancakes

In Ireland, because traditionally eggs and milk were not used during Lent, any eggs or milk that were in the house were used for special pancakes for Shrove Tuesday, the day before Ash Wednesday.

- 2 cups all-purpose flour
- 2 teaspoons baking soda
- 2 teaspoons granulated sugar
- ½ teaspoon salt
- 2 medium eggs, lightly beaten, or equivalent egg substitute
- 3 tablespoons canola oil
- 2 cups fat-free buttermilk (or 2 cups 1% lowfat milk mixed with 2 tablespoons white vinegar)
- ½ cup frozen lowfat non-dairy whipped topping, thawed, for serving (optional)
- Berries, for garnish (optional)

Sift the flour, baking soda, sugar, and salt together into a large bowl. In a separate bowl, beat the eggs, oil, and buttermilk together. Add the wet ingredients to the dry ingredients and combine thoroughly but don't overmix; allow small lumps to remain.

Lightly oil a frying pan or griddle and heat over medium heat until a drop of water will dance on it. Pour ⅓ cup of the batter onto the griddle and cook until golden on the bottom and evenly covered with bubbles on the top, about 2 minutes. Flip and cook on the other side, until lightly browned. Top with whipped topping and berries, if desired.

YIELD: *14 pancakes* EACH SERVING CONTAINS: *Carbohydrates:* 16 grams *Calories:* 116

polish cottage cheese
and pear snacks

This is a very quick dessert to make because the cake is actually pancakes.

1 (10-ounce) can unsweetened pear halves in juice
1 cup all-purpose flour
½ teaspoon baking soda
¼ teaspoon salt
1 tablespoon granulated sugar
1 large egg, beaten
1 cup 1% lowfat milk
1 tablespoon white vinegar
2 cups lowfat small curd cottage cheese

Drain the pear halves. Combine the flour, baking soda, salt, and sugar in a large bowl. Combine the egg, milk, and vinegar in a small bowl. Add the milk mixture to the flour mixture and beat until smooth.

Spray a skillet or griddle with nonstick cooking spray and heat over medium heat until it is hot enough for a bead of water dropped on the surface to dance. Ladle enough batter onto the hot surface to make a small pancake. Cook until the top is covered with bubbles, then turn and cook on the other side. Repeat, using the remaining batter. Stack the pancakes, alternating each with a layer of cottage cheese. Arrange the pear halves in a fan shape on top of the stack. Cut into wedges and serve.

YIELD: *8 servings* EACH SERVING CONTAINS: *Carbohydrates:* 11 grams *Calories:* 166

roll-ups

basic roll-up

U se this for all the jelly roll–style recipes that follow.

1 cup cake flour
1 teaspoon baking powder
3 large eggs
¼ cup granulated sugar
3 packages sugar substitute
⅓ cup water
1 teaspoon vanilla extract

Preheat the oven to 375°F. Spray a 15 x 10½ x 1-inch jelly-roll pan with non-stick cooking spray. Line the bottom with wax paper, then spray the paper.

Sift the flour and baking powder into a medium bowl. In a medium bowl, using an electric mixer at high speed, beat the eggs until thick and creamy and light in color. Gradually add the sugar and sugar substitute, beating constantly until the mixture is very thick. Stir in the water and vanilla, then fold in the flour mixture. Spread the batter evenly in the prepared pan.

Bake 12 minutes, or until the center of the cake springs back when lightly pressed. Loosen the cake around the edges with a knife, invert the pan onto a clean kitchen towel, and peel off the wax paper. Starting at the short end, roll up the cake and towel together. Place the roll seam side down on a wire rack and cool completely. Carefully unroll, add the filling, and roll it up according to the individual recipe. Using a sharp knife, evenly score where you will later slice the roll-up.

YIELD: *10 slices* EACH SLICE CONTAINS: *Carbohydrates:* 14 grams *Calories:* 82

fresh strawberry roll-up

This is my friend Annette's new substitute for strawberry short-cake—it was a hit at her Fourth of July cookout.

1 recipe Basic Roll-Up (page 146)
2 cups frozen lowfat non-dairy whipped topping, thawed
2 cups hulled and quartered fresh strawberries

Prepare the Basic Roll-Up recipe. Cool and unroll. In a medium bowl combine the whipped topping and the strawberries. Spread the filling evenly over the roll.

Starting from the short end, roll up the cake by lifting the cake with the end of the towel. Place the roll seam side down on a serving plate. Cut into 1-inch slices.

YIELD: *10 slices* EACH SLICE CONTAINS: *Carbohydrates:* 19 grams *Calories:* 96

peach melba roll-up

S ince this recipe uses canned peaches, you can make it off the shelf anytime.

1 recipe Basic Roll-Up (page 146)
1 recipe Vanilla Tart Filling (page 38)
15 ounces unsweetened sliced peaches in juice, drained

Prepare the Basic Roll-Up recipe. Cool and unroll. Prepare the tart filling and stir in the peaches. Spread the filling evenly over the roll.

Starting from the short end, roll up the cake by lifting the cake with the end of the towel. Place the roll seam side down on a serving plate. Cut into 1-inch slices before serving.

YIELD: *10 slices* EACH SLICE CONTAINS: *Carbohydrates:* 26 grams *Calories:* 164

banana walnut roll-up

I f you like banana bread, this has the same flavor but is lighter and lower in carbs.

1 recipe Basic Roll-Up (page 146)
1 recipe Vanilla Tart Filling (page 38)
3 small ripe bananas, peeled and sliced
¼ cup chopped walnuts

Prepare the Basic Roll-Up recipe. Cool and unroll. Prepare the tart filling and stir in the bananas and walnuts. Spread the filling evenly over the roll.

Starting from the short end, roll up the cake by lifting the cake with the end of the towel. Place the roll seam side down on a serving plate. Cut into 1-inch slices.

YIELD: *10 slices* EACH SLICE CONTAINS: *Carbohydrates:* 29 grams *Calories:* 195

mocha raspberry roll-up

A very elegant and grown-up taste.

1 recipe Basic Roll-Up (page 146)
1 recipe Mocha Tart Filling (see below)
2 cups fresh raspberries

MOCHA TART FILLING
1 package (4 servings) sugar-free chocolate pudding mix
1½ cups skim milk
1 tablespoon instant coffee powder (or instant espresso
coffee powder for a sharper coffee taste)

Prepare the Basic Roll-Up recipe. Cool and unroll.

To make the filling, combine the pudding mix, milk, and coffee powder in a medium saucepan over medium heat. Bring to a boil and cook, stirring constantly, until the pudding has thickened. Cool and stir in the raspberries. Spread the filling evenly over the roll.

Starting from the short end, roll up the cake by lifting the cake with the end of the towel. Place the roll seam side down on a serving plate. Cut into 1-inch slices.

YIELD: *10 slices* EACH SLICE CONTAINS: *Carbohydrates:* 17 grams *Calories:* 96

pistachio pineapple roll-up

T he pineapple adds lightness to the pistachio pudding mix.

1 recipe Basic Roll-Up (page 146)
1 package (4 servings) sugar-free instant pistachio pudding
1¾ cups skim milk
1 cup crushed pineapple in juice, drained

Prepare the Basic Roll-Up recipe. Cool and unroll. Put the pudding mix into a mixing bowl. Add the milk and mix until the pudding is thick. Beat in the pineapple. Spread the filling evenly over the roll.

Starting from the short end, roll up the cake by lifting the cake with the end of the towel. Place the roll seam side down on a serving plate. Cut into 1-inch slices.

YIELD: *10 slices* EACH SLICE CONTAINS: *Carbohydrates:* 21 grams *Calories:* 114

apricot roll-up

I love to serve this after a big salad meal. It's light and sweet.

1 recipe Basic Roll-Up (page 146)
½ cup all-fruit apricot preserves
¼ cup water

Prepare the Basic Roll-Up recipe. Cool and unroll. In a small saucepan over low heat, combine the preserves and water and stir until smooth. Spread the filling evenly over the roll.

Starting from the short end, roll up the cake by lifting the cake with the end of the towel. Place the roll seam side down on a serving plate. Cut into 1-inch slices.

YIELD: *10 slices* EACH SLICE CONTAINS: *Carbohydrates:* 21 grams *Calories:* 111

meringues

The recipes in this chapter are all based on meringue-beaten egg whites that are slowly baked. They are low in fat and very elegant. You might think meringues are beyond your capabilities—they are not! It's hard to go wrong if you follow a few simple rules.

- Don't beat the egg whites in plastic. Glass or metal bowls will give your whites the greatest volume.

- Make sure your utensils are spotless. Your bowls, blades, and scrapers should be grease-free.

- Don't allow bits of yolk to mix in with the whites. Separate whites and yolks into small cups or bowls, one at a time, and put only clean egg whites in the mixing bowl.

- Recognize that humidity changes meringues. On high humidity days, meringues are chewy. On low humidity days, meringues are dry and crisp.

- Never open the oven, even to peek, until the time called for in the recipe has elapsed.

- Use reconstituted Just Whites powdered egg whites if you have no use for leftover yolks. They can be found in supermarkets, health food stores, or gourmet shops.

- Even though egg substitutes are mostly egg whites, they won't work in meringues.

- Freeze meringues after you've made them or store them at room temperature in an airtight container.

basic meringue

Follow the tips on page 154 for best results.

3 large egg whites
¼ teaspoon cream of tartar
¼ cup granulated sugar

Preheat the oven to 250°F. or the temperature specified in the specific recipe. Cut a brown paper bag or parchment paper to fit over a cookie sheet. Using plates, cups, or saucers and a pencil, trace the shape specified in the recipe onto the paper. In a large glass or metal bowl, use an electric mixer on medium speed to beat the egg whites with the cream of tartar. When soft peaks begin to form, keep beating and slowly add the sugar. Increase the mixer's speed to high and beat until stiff peaks form and the meringue is glossy. Don't beat past this point or the meringue will become too dry!

With a clean spoon or rubber scraper transfer the beaten egg white to the circles drawn on the paper. Bake for the amount of time specified in the recipe. When the time is up, turn off the oven but don't open the oven door. Leave the meringues in the turned-off oven for 2 more hours, then carefully remove the cookie sheets from the oven and use a spatula to loosen the meringue from the paper. Store meringue in an airtight container with waxed paper between each one. In damp weather, meringue is chewy.

YIELD: *1 Basic Meringue recipe (4 servings)* EACH SERVING CONTAINS: *Carbohydrates:* 13 grams *Calories:* 61

lime kisses

My daughters, Anna and Adie call these Surprise Kisses and they love them because of the sparkly sensation you get in your mouth when you eat them.

1 recipe Basic Meringue (page 155)
1 package (4 servings) sugar-free lime gelatin mix

Preheat the oven to 275°F. Prepare the Basic Meringue recipe, adding the lime gelatin when you add the sugar. Cut a brown paper bag or parchment paper to fit over a cookie sheet. Drop the meringue by the teaspoon onto the cookie sheet.

Bake for 30 minutes. Turn off the oven. Leave the kisses in the oven for another 10 minutes without opening the door. Use a spatula to remove the kisses from the paper. Store in an airtight container. Meringue is more chewy in damp weather.

YIELD: *5 dozen kisses* EACH KISS CONTAINS: *Carbohydrates:* 1 grams *Calories:* 4

tart orange meringue tarts

T hin slices of orange give this tart a festive garnish.

1 recipe Basic Meringue (page 155)
2 tablespoons granulated sugar
4 teaspoons cornstarch
1 cup orange juice
1 tablespoon lemon juice (fresh is best)
1 teaspoon sugar substitute
½ cup frozen lowfat non-dairy whipped topping, thawed (optional)

Preheat the oven to 250°F. Prepare the Basic Meringue recipe. Cut a brown paper bag or parchment paper to fit over a cookie sheet. Draw six 4-inch circles on the paper. Spoon the meringue into the circles, building up the edges by an inch, and form a depression in the middle to make a tart shell.

Bake for 1 hour. Turn off the oven. Leave the tarts in the oven for another 2 hours without opening the door. Use a spatula to remove the tarts from the paper. Store in a dry place. If you need to store them for more than an hour or two before serving, put them in an airtight container.

While the meringues are in the oven, prepare the filling by combining the sugar and cornstarch in a medium saucepan over medium heat. Whisk in the orange juice. Cook, stirring constantly, until the mixture thickens, about 3 minutes. Remove from the heat and stir in the lemon juice and sugar substitute. Cool and keep in the refrigerator until just before serving.

To serve, spoon the filling into the meringue shells and top with a dollop of your favorite whipped topping, if desired.

YIELD: *6 tarts* EACH TART CONTAINS: *Carbohydrates:* 19 grams *Calories:* 84

tangerine cream tarts

These tarts are great in the winter when tangerines are at their sweetest.

1 recipe Basic Meringue (page 155)
1 cup fat-free cream cheese
3 tablespoons Triple Sec
4 teaspoons cornstarch
1⅓ cups unsweetened orange or tangerine juice
(frozen concentrate is okay)
3 tangerines, peeled, separated into segments, and pitted

Preheat oven to 250°F. Prepare the Basic Meringue Recipe (page 155). Cut a brown paper bag or parchment paper to fit over a cookie sheet. Draw six 4-inch circles on the paper. Spoon the meringue into the circles, building up the edges by an inch, and form a depression in the middle to make a tart shell.

Bake for 1 hour. Turn off the oven. Leave the tarts in the oven for another 2 hours without opening the door. Use a spatula to remove the tarts from the paper. Store in a dry place. If you need to store them for more than an hour or two before serving, put them in an airtight container.

While the meringues are in the oven, prepare the filling by combining the orange juice, cornstarch and Triple Sec in a saucepan over medium heat until the mixture thickens. Beat in cream cheese a spoonful at a time using a whisk or electric mixer. Cool and keep in the refrigerator until just before serving. To serve, spoon the filling onto the meringue shells. Top with tangerine sections.

YIELD: *6 tarts* EACH TART CONTAINS: *Carbohydrates: 26 grams Calories: 151*

traditional pavlova

This lovely dessert was created for the graceful Russian ballerina Anna Pavlova when she visited New Zealand and Australia in the early 1900s.

1 recipe Basic Meringue (page 155)
2 cups frozen lowfat non-dairy whipped topping, thawed
2 cups hulled fresh strawberries, sliced lengthwise
4 ripe kiwis, peeled and sliced into coins

Preheat the oven to 250°F. Prepare the Basic Meringue recipe. Cut a brown paper bag or parchment paper to fit over a cookie sheet. Trace a 12-inch circle on the paper. Spoon the meringue into the circle, spreading it so it is evenly distributed. Bake for 1 hour. Turn off the oven. Leave the meringue in the oven for another 30 minutes without opening the door. Cool on a wire rack.

Carefully separate the meringue from the paper and place the meringue on a serving plate. Just before serving, spread the whipped topping carefully over the top of the meringue. Place the strawberries on top, cut-side-down, with the points extending out past the edge of the meringue. Arrange the kiwis inside the strawberries, overlapping them to form a ring. Arrange any remaining strawberries in the center of the circles.

YIELD: *10 servings* EACH SERVING CONTAINS: *Carbohydrates:* 15 grams *Calories:* 84

pavlova wedges with kiwis and raspberry sauce

A variation of the traditional Pavlova that makes individual servings.

1 recipe Basic Meringue (page 155)
4 ripe kiwis, peeled and thinly sliced
1 recipe Raspberry Sauce (page 30)

Preheat the oven to 250°F. Prepare the Basic Meringue recipe. Cut a brown paper bag or parchment paper to fit over a cookie sheet. Trace a 12-inch circle on the paper. Spoon the meringue into the circle, spreading it so it is evenly distributed.

Bake for 1 hour. Turn off the oven. Leave the meringue in the oven for another 30 minutes without opening the door to cool. Using a spatula, lift meringue to a flat surface.

Carefully cut the meringue into 8 wedges. Place each wedge on a dessert plate. Arrange half of a sliced kiwi on each meringue wedge. Spoon raspberry sauce on top and serve.

YIELD: *8 servings* EACH SERVING CONTAINS: *Carbohydrates:* 21 grams *Calories:* 98

hungarian fruit cream

Y ou can use any fresh berries in season for this fruit cream.

¾ cup 1% lowfat milk
4 tablespoons granulated sugar
2 large egg yolks
1 envelope unflavored gelatin
2 tablespoons hot water
½ cup pureed berries
2 cups frozen lowfat non-dairy whipped topping, thawed

Combine the milk with 2 tablespoons of the sugar in a small saucepan over medium heat and bring to a boil. In the top of a double boiler over simmering water, whip the egg yolks with the remaining 2 tablespoons of the sugar. While continuing to whip, add the hot milk. Stir until the mixture thickens into a custard, about 5 minutes. Remove from heat and continue stirring until luke-warm. Sprinkle the gelatin on top of the mixture and stir until well mixed. Add the berry puree and fold in the whipped topping.

Spoon into 6 dessert glasses. Cover and place in the refrigerator to chill until set, about 3 to 5 hours, before serving.

YIELD: *6 servings* EACH SERVING CONTAINS: *Carbohydrates:* 17 grams *Calories:* 161

danish rice and almond dessert

A traditional Scandinavian Christmas dessert.

4 cups 1% lowfat milk
3 tablespoons granulated sugar
¾ cup long grain rice
½ cup blanched and chopped almonds
¼ cup sherry or unsweetened apple juice
2 teaspoons vanilla extract

Place the milk in a 2-quart saucepan over medium heat, then add the sugar and rice. Bring to a boil, stirring once or twice, then lower the heat and simmer, uncovered, for 25 minutes, or until the rice is soft. Pour into a shallow bowl and add the chopped almonds, sherry, and vanilla. Cool before serving. This is usually served slightly warm the first time. Leftovers (if there are any) should be covered and refrigerated. Subsequent servings, then, are cold.

YIELD: *10 servings* EACH SERVING CONTAINS: *Carbohydrates:* 19 grams *Calories:* 142

hawaiian sweet potato pudding

This is a real treat. Even people who aren't crazy about sweet potatoes love this. If you are using canned or leftover sweet potatoes, start with the second step.

3 medium sweet potatoes, peeled and sliced
2½ cups tightly packed coconut flakes
1½ cups 1% lowfat milk

Place the sweet potatoes in a large pot of water and bring to a boil. Lower the heat and simmer until soft. Drain and mash with a fork or process in a food processor.

Place the mashed sweet potatoes in a large saucepan over medium heat and add the coconut flakes and milk. Cook, stirring frequently, until the pudding has the consistency of a thick batter, about 10 minutes. Serve hot or cold.

YIELD: *8 servings* EACH SERVING CONTAINS: *Carbohydrates:* 25 grams *Calories:* 280

chinese almond cream

You might like to try 3 tablespoons of Amaretto in place of the almond extract.

4 cups 1% lowfat milk
1 cup almonds, blanched
¼ cup granulated sugar
¼ cup rice flour
½ teaspoon almond extract
1 cup fresh strawberries or other berries, for serving

Place 3½ cups of the milk in a large saucepan over medium-low heat. Add the almonds and sugar and bring to a boil, stirring occasionally. Remove from the heat, cover, and let stand for 45 minutes. Strain the mixture through a colander set over a bowl. Using the back of a wooden spoon, press down hard on the almonds to force them through the holes. Discard the hard pieces of almond that don't fit. Return the liquid to the saucepan.

In a small bowl, combine the rice flour with the remaining ½ cup milk and pour it into the saucepan and return to low heat. Simmer for about 15 minutes, stirring frequently, or until the custard is thick enough to coat a spoon. Stir in the almond extract.

Spoon into a serving bowl. Cover with plastic wrap and place in the refrigerator to chill for at least 2 hours before serving. Serve garnished with berries.

YIELD: *10 servings* EACH SERVING CONTAINS: *Carbohydrates:* 16 grams *Calories:* 164

british queen of puddings

This baked pudding has a meringue crown—that's why it's the queen!

Peel from 1 lemon, cut in pieces
2 cups 1% lowfat milk
2 tablespoons unsalted butter
¼ cup plus 2 tablespoons granulated sugar
1 cup fresh white breadcrumbs (remove the crusts and pulverize the bread in a blender)
3 large eggs, separated
¼ cup all-fruit raspberry jam

Preheat the oven to 350°F. Grease a 9-inch pie pan well.

Place the lemon peel and milk in a large heavy saucepan over low heat, bring to a simmer, and simmer for 4 to 5 minutes. Remove the peel and discard it. Add the butter and ¼ cup of the sugar, gradually increase the heat to medium and cook, stirring constantly, until the sugar dissolves. Remove from the heat and stir in the breadcrumbs. Set aside to cool. Beat in the egg yolks.

Pour the mixture into the prepared pie pan and smooth the top. Bake for 20 minutes, or until the pudding is firm. Place on a rack to cool.

Beat the egg whites in a large bowl until foamy. Add the remaining 2 tablespoons sugar and beat until stiff peaks form. Melt the jam in a small saucepan over low heat. Pour the jam evenly over the cooled pudding. Carefully spoon the egg whites over the jam.

Return to the oven and bake for 10 to 12 minutes, or until the top is golden brown.

YIELD: *8 servings* EACH SERVING CONTAINS: *Carbohydrates:* 26 grams *Calories:* 199

french raspberry pavlova

You will be a hit with everyone when you serve this. My family loves the refrigerated leftovers for breakfast!

1 recipe Basic Meringue (page 155)
1 recipe Vanilla Tart Filling (page 38)
2 cups fresh raspberries

Preheat the oven to 250°F. Prepare the Basic Meringue recipe. Cut a brown paper bag or parchment paper to fit over a cookie sheet. Trace a 12-inch circle on the paper. Spoon the meringue into the circle, spreading it so it is evenly distributed.

Bake for 1 hour. Turn off the oven. Leave the meringue in the oven for another 30 minutes without opening the door. Remove to a wire rack to cool.

While the meringue is baking, prepare the Vanilla Tart Filling and allow it to cool. Carefully separate the meringue from the paper using a spatula. Place the meringue on a serving plate. Spoon on the filling, smoothing it evenly to the edges. Arrange the raspberries on top in concentric circles, beginning at the outside edge. Serve immediately.

YIELD: *10 servings* EACH SERVING CONTAINS: *Carbohydrates:* 15 grams *Calories:* 100

peach pavlova

This Pavlova is topped with ice cream or frozen yogurt. The combination of chewy meringue and soft and creamy ice cream is delightful.

1 recipe Basic Meringue (page 155)
2 cups sugar-free fat-free vanilla ice cream or frozen yogurt, softened
15 ounces unsweetened peach slices in juice, drained

Preheat the oven to 250°F. Prepare the Basic Meringue recipe. Cut a brown paper bag or parchment paper to fit over a cookie sheet. Trace a 12-inch circle on the paper. Spoon the meringue into the circle, spreading it so it is evenly distributed. Bake for 1 hour. Turn off the oven. Leave the meringue in the oven for an additional 30 minutes without opening the door. Remove to a wire rack to cool.

Carefully separate the meringue from the paper using a spatula. Place the meringue on a serving plate. Just before serving, spread the ice cream over the meringue and arrange peach slices in a circle at the edge. Place any remaining peach slices in the center.

YIELD: *10 servings* EACH SERVING CONTAINS: *Carbohydrates:* 18 grams *Calories:* 83

lemon meringue kisses

U se a pastry bag with a ½-inch star tip for even, professional looking kisses.

1 recipe Basic Meringue (page 155)
2 teaspoons finely grated lemon zest
½ teaspoon lemon extract

Preheat the oven to 250°F. Prepare the Basic Meringue with the following adap-
tion: After the egg whites form peaks, quickly beat in the lemon zest and lemon
extract. Cut a brown paper bag or parchment paper to fit over cookie sheets.
Drop the meringues by teaspoonfuls onto the paper. Bake for 40 minutes. Turn
off the oven. Leave the meringues in the oven for an additional 5 minutes without opening the door. Remove from the oven and cool for a minute or two.
Remove to a wire rack to cool completely. Use a spatula to separate the
meringues from the paper.

YIELD: *5 dozen kisses* EACH KISS CONTAINS: *Carbohydrates:* 1 grams *Calories:* 4

double meringue
butterscotch pie

There is meringue on the bottom (chunky), butterscotch in the middle (creamy and smooth), and meringue on top (chewy)—something for everyone.

1 recipe Basic Meringue (page 155), using 4 egg whites
1 package (4 servings) sugar-free butterscotch pudding mix
(not instant)
2 cups skim milk

Preheat the oven to 250°F. Coat a 10-inch pie pan with nonstick cooking spray.

Prepare the Basic Meringue with the 4 egg whites and smooth two-thirds of the meringue onto the inside of the pie pan. Shape the meringue into the shape of the pie pan. Keep the remaining meringue in the refrigerator.

Bake for 1 hour. Turn off the oven. Leave the pie crust in the oven for another 30 minutes. When you remove the meringue from the oven, turn the oven to 350°F.

Meanwhile, prepare the pudding according to package directions using the skim milk. Just before serving, spoon the pudding into the shell and cover with remaining uncooked meringue, making sure the meringue topping covers the crust all the way around. Use a spoon to form peaks.

Bake for 10 to 15 minutes, or until the topping is lightly browned. Cool on a wire rack. Use a knife that you have run under hot water to cut each sheet.

YIELD: *8 servings* EACH SERVING CONTAINS: *Carbohydrates:* 10 grams *Calories:* 54

meringue chantilly

T ry putting a few drops of food coloring in the whipped topping to match a party color scheme.

1 recipe Basic Meringue (page 155)
2 cups frozen lowfat non-dairy whipped topping, thawed

Preheat the oven to 275°F. Prepare the Basic Meringue recipe. Cut brown paper bags or parchment paper to fit over 2 cookie sheets. Spoon the meringue onto the paper to make 12 mounds.

Bake for 30 minutes. Open the oven door and reverse the positions of the cookie sheets. Bake for another 30 minutes. Remove the cookie sheets from the oven. Loosen and turn each meringue over. Gently depress the center of each one with the back of a spoon. Return to the oven and bake 30 more minutes. Remove from oven and place the meringues on racks to cool completely. Just before serving, make sandwiches by placing the whipped topping in between two meringues.

YIELD: *6 servings* EACH SERVING CONTAINS: *Carbohydrates:* 14 grams *Calories:* 94

schaum torte

T his is a great strawberry shortcake replacement.

1 recipe Basic Meringue (page 155)
1 tablespoon granulated sugar
2¼ cups sliced fresh or frozen and thawed unsweetened
   whole strawberries
1 cup frozen lowfat non-dairy whipped topping, thawed
9 hulled whole strawberries, for garnish

Preheat the oven to 275°F. Prepare the Basic Meringue recipe. Cut brown paper bags or parchment paper to fit over 2 cookie sheets. Drop meringue onto the paper, making 9 mounds. Use a tablespoon dipped in cold water to make an indentation in the top of each mound.

Bake for 45 minutes. Turn off the oven, keep the door closed and wait 30 minutes before removing the meringues from the oven. Remove and place onto wire racks to cool thoroughly.

Meanwhile, in a small bowl, sprinkle the sugar over the sliced strawberries, stir, and let stand.

To assemble, place the meringues on dessert plates and scoop strawberries into the indentation. Top with a dollop of whipped topping and garnish with a whole strawberry.

YIELD: *8 servings* EACH SERVING CONTAINS: *Carbohydrates:* 14 grams *Calories:* 72

strawberry bombe

In the same class as Baked Alaska. Prepare this for a crowd.

1 recipe Baked Meringue (page 155)
1 quart sugar-free fat-free strawberry ice cream
1 teaspoon vanilla extract

Preheat the oven to 275°F. Prepare Basic Meringue recipe. Cut a brown paper bag or parchment paper to fit over a cookie sheet. Trace a 9-inch circle on the paper. Smooth one-third of the meringue inside the circle and bake for 30 minutes. Turn off the oven but do not open the door. Leave the meringue in the oven for another 20 minutes. Remove to a wire rack to cool but do not remove the paper until completely cool. Just before serving, preheat the oven to 450°F.

Heap the ice cream carefully in a mound on the meringue. Beat the vanilla into the remaining uncooked meringue. Smooth the uncooked meringue evenly over the strawberry ice cream dome, making sure it touches the baked meringue at all points.

Bake until the meringue is a delicate brown, about 3 minutes. Serve right away, being careful to cut the meringue away from the brown paper.

YIELD: *8 servings* EACH SERVING CONTAINS: *Carbohydrates:* 27 grams *Calories:* 131

chocolate dream torte

A pile of meringues and fillings. Kajsa, my oldest daughter, likes it best after the meringue has been refrigerated for a few hours and gets chewy.

1 recipe Basic Meringue (page 155)
1 package (4 servings) sugar-free chocolate pudding mix
1¼ cups frozen lowfat non-dairy whipped topping, thawed

Preheat the oven to 250°F. Prepare the Basic Meringue recipe. Cut brown paper bags or parchment paper to fit over 3 cookie sheets. Trace an 8-inch pie pan 3 times. Distribute the meringue among the 3 circles and smooth it evenly.

Bake for 40 minutes. Turn off the oven. Leave the meringue in the oven for another 30 minutes without opening the door. Remove to wire racks to cool.

When you are ready to assemble the torte, carefully remove one of the meringues from the paper and place it on a serving plate. Prepare the pudding according to package directions using water or skim milk. (Skim milk will increase carbs a bit, but give you protein and calcium as well as some vitamins.) Cool if it is not instant pudding. Place half the pudding on one meringue, smoothing to the edges. Place a second meringue (with paper removed) on top and repeat with the last of the pudding and top with the third meringue. Cut carefully and top each serving with a dollop of whipped topping.

YIELD: *8 servings* EACH SERVING CONTAINS: *Carbohydrates:* 12 grams *Calories:* 74

creamsicle gelatin

Do you love creamsicles? This recipe will get you close in taste for very few carbs!

1 package (4 servings) sugar-free orange gelatin mix
1 cup boiling water
½ cup sugar-free lowfat vanilla ice cream
½ cup cold water
¼ cup orange sections

Place the gelatin in a large bowl. Add the boiling water and stir until the gelatin is dissolved. Add the ice cream and cold water and stir to mix. Pour into 4 dessert bowls. Cover and place in the refrigerator to chill until firm, 3 to 4 hours before serving. Serve garnished with the orange sections.

YIELD: *4 servings* EACH SERVING CONTAINS: *Carbohydrates: 6 grams Calories: 22*

cream puffs

cream puff pastry

You won't believe how easy cream puffs are to make until you prepare them yourself. This recipe is practically foolproof and needs no special kitchen equipment.

1 cup water
⅓ cup canola oil
1 cup all-purpose flour
4 large eggs or equivalent egg substitute
1 teaspoon butter-flavored extract
1 teaspoon vanilla extract

Preheat the oven to 400°F. Combine the water and oil in a medium saucepan over high heat and bring to a rolling boil. Lower the heat to low and add the flour all at once, stirring with a wooden spoon until the mixture forms a ball. Remove from the heat. Using an electric mixer at medium speed, beat in the eggs one at a time. Add the butter-flavored and vanilla extracts. Using a spoon, drop 12 spoonfuls of batter onto an ungreased cookie sheet.

Bake for 10 minutes. Puffs will be golden brown when done. Reduce the heat to 350°F and bake for 25 minutes longer. Turn off the oven but do not remove cream puffs until they are quite firm to the touch. Remove from the oven and cool on wire racks away from drafts. Use a sharp knife to cut the puffs horizontally. If you find any damp dough remaining inside, scoop it out before filling.

Fill and serve the cream puffs according to the recipes that follow.

YIELD: *12 cream puffs* EACH CREAM PUFF CONTAINS: *Carbohydrates:* 8 grams *Calories:* 117

light chocolate cream puffs

V ery impressive, and easier than pie!

1 recipe Cream Puff Pastry (page 176)
1 recipe Chocolate Mousse Pudding (page 116)
1 recipe Chocolate Glaze (page 30)

Prepare the Cream Puff Pastry recipe. While the pastry is in the oven, make the Chocolate Mousse Pudding and the Chocolate Glaze or Fudge Topping.

To assemble, spoon the Chocolate Mousse Pudding into the cream puffs, replace the tops, and drizzle Chocolate Glaze on top. Serve immediately.

YIELD: *12 cream puffs* EACH CREAM PUFF CONTAINS: *Carbohydrates:* 11 grams *Calories:* 139

light mocha cream puffs

For those who love that mocha flavor.

1 recipe Cream Puff Pastry (page 176)
1 recipe Mocha Tart Filling (page 150)
1 recipe Chocolate Glaze (page 30)

Prepare the Cream Puff Pastry recipe. While the pastry is in the oven, make the Mocha Tart Filling.

To assemble, spoon the Mocha Tart Filling into the cream puffs, replace the tops, and drizzle Chocolate Glaze on top. Serve immediately.

YIELD: *12 cream puffs* EACH CREAM PUFF CONTAINS: *Carbohydrates:* 10 grams *Calories:* 125

traditional cream puffs

Th:hese will look and taste just as the cream puffs sold in fine bakeries.

1 recipe Cream Puff Pastry (page 176)
1 recipe Vanilla Tart Filling (page 38)
1 recipe Chocolate Glaze (page 30) or
    Napoleon Fudge Topping (page 31)

Prepare the Cream Puff Pastry recipe. While the pastry is in the oven, make the Vanilla Tart Filling and the Chocolate Glaze.

To assemble, spoon Vanilla Tart Filling into the cream puffs, replace the tops, and drizzle Chocolate Glaze or Napoleon Fudge on top. Serve immediately.

YIELD: *12 cream puffs* EACH CREAM PUFF CONTAINS: *Carbohydrates:* 15 grams *Calories:* 176

mocha cream puffs

These have a more pronounced coffee flavor than the Light Mocha Cream Puffs on page 178.

1 recipe Cream Puff Pastry (page 176)
1 recipe Mocha Tart Filling (page 150)
1 recipe Mocha Glaze (page 32)

Prepare the Cream Puff Pastry recipe. While the pastry is in the oven, make the Mocha Tart Filling and the Mocha Glaze.

To assemble, spoon Mocha Tart Filling into the cream puffs, replace the tops, and drizzle Mocha Glaze on top. Serve immediately.

YIELD: *12 cream puffs* EACH CREAM PUFF CONTAINS: *Carbohydrates:* 10 grams *Calories:* 125

strawberry cream puffs

An easy and very attractive alternative to strawberry shortcake.

1 recipe Cream Puff Pastry (page 176)
3 cups fresh or frozen and thawed whole unsweetened strawberries
1 cup frozen lowfat non-dairy whipped topping, thawed

Prepare the Cream Puff Pastry recipe. To assemble, fill each puff with ¼ cup of the strawberries. Replace the top and top with a dollop of whipped topping. Serve immediately.

YIELD: *12 cream puffs* EACH CREAM PUFF CONTAINS: *Carbohydrates:* 12 grams *Calories:* 142

banana cream puffs

If you have bananas, all the rest of the ingredients should be on the shelf. This is great to make for unexpected guests.

1 recipe Cream Puff Pastry (page 176)
1 recipe Vanilla Tart Filling (page 38)
4 medium bananas, peeled and sliced
1 tablespoon lemon juice
1 cup frozen lowfat non-dairy whipped topping, thawed

Prepare the Cream Puff Pastry recipe. While the pastry is in the oven, make the Vanilla Tart Filling. Place the banana slices in a medium bowl. Pour the lemon juice over the bananas and toss to distribute the lemon juice evenly. Stir in the Vanilla Tart Filling.

To assemble, spoon the pudding mixture into the cream puffs. Replace the tops and top with a dollop of whipped topping. Serve immediately.

YIELD: *12 cream puffs* EACH CREAM PUFF CONTAINS: *Carbohydrates:* 24 grams *Calories:* 216

cream puffs with
raspberry sauce

T he raspberry sauce looks striking against the light-colored cream puffs and filling, and it also adds a contrasting flavor and texture.

1 recipe Cream Puff Pastry (page 176)
1 recipe Vanilla Tart Filling (page 38)
1 recipe Raspberry Sauce (page 30)

Prepare the Cream Puff Pastry recipe. While the pastry is in the oven, prepare the Vanilla Tart Filling and Raspberry Sauce.

To assemble, spoon the Vanilla Tart Filling into the cream puffs and replace the tops. Spoon the Raspberry Sauce over the cream puffs and serve immediately.

YIELD: *12 cream puffs* EACH CREAM PUFF CONTAINS: *Carbohydrates:* 20 grams *Calories:* 199

new zealand cream puffs

K iwis are ready to use when they yield to gentle pressure. Eat them at their sweetest.

1 recipe Cream Puff Pastry (page 176)
4 kiwis, peeled and chopped
2 cups hulled and sliced fresh strawberries
2 cups frozen lowfat non-dairy whipped topping, thawed

Prepare the Cream Puff Pastry recipe. When ready to assemble, combine the kiwis and strawberries in a large bowl. Fold in the whipped topping. Spoon the fruit mixture into the cream puffs. Replace the tops and serve immediately.

YIELD: *12 cream puffs* EACH CREAM PUFF CONTAINS: *Carbohydrates:* 16 grams *Calories:* 167

icy peach cream puffs

Bake the cream puffs and refrigerate the peaches in the morning. Assemble just before serving.

1 recipe Cream Puff Pastry (page 176)
3 cups sugar-free lowfat vanilla ice cream or frozen yogurt
30 ounces canned peaches packed in juice, drained,
 chopped, and chilled

Prepare the Cream Puff Pastry recipe. When ready to serve, fill each cream puff with ¼ cup ice cream. Distribute the chopped peaches over the ice cream. Replace the tops and serve immediately.

YIELD: *12 cream puffs* EACH CREAM PUFF CONTAINS: *Carbohydrates:* 22 grams *Calories:* 172

frozen chocolate cream puffs

P repare these ahead of time and freeze them. I move them to the refrigerator just as I'm putting dinner on the table.

1 recipe Cream Puff Pastry (page 176)
3 cups skim milk, chilled
2 packages (4 servings) sugar-free chocolate pudding mix

Prepare the Cream Puff Pastry recipe. While the pastry is in the oven, in a medium bowl, using an electric mixer on high speed, beat together the milk and the pudding mix until thick.

To assemble, spoon the pudding into the cream puffs, replace the tops, and place them in the freezer. When they have frozen, store them in plastic freezer bags in the freezer until you are ready to use them.

YIELD: *12 cream puffs* EACH CREAM PUFF CONTAINS: *Carbohydrates:* 12 grams *Calories:* 141

frozen raspberry cream puffs

These make-ahead cream puffs freeze perfectly so you can eat one at a time.

1 recipe Cream Puff Pastry (page 176)
1 recipe raspberry filling for Raspberry Cream Pie (page 68)

Prepare the Cream Puff Pastry recipe. While the pastry is in the oven, prepare the Raspberry Filling.

To assemble, spoon the filling into the cream puffs, replace the tops, and place them in the freezer. When they have frozen, store them in plastic freezer bags in the freezer. Remove from the freezer just before dinner and they will be ready by dessert time.

YIELD: *12 cream puffs* EACH CREAM PUFF CONTAINS: *Carbohydrates:* 15 grams *Calories:* 156

frozen strawberry cream puffs

Remove as many as you need from the freezer as you get dinner ready. I make these on rainy Sunday afternoons and serve them on weeknights to follow rushed after-work dinners.

1 recipe Cream Puff Pastry (page 176)
1 recipe Strawberry Ice Cream Pie Filling (page 71)

Prepare the Cream Puff Pastry recipe. While the pastry is in the oven, make the Strawberry Ice Cream Pie Filling.

To assemble, spoon the filling into the cream puffs, replace the tops, and place them in the freezer. When they have frozen, store them in plastic freezer bags n the freezer until you are ready to use them.

YIELD: *12 cream puffs* EACH CREAM PUFF CONTAINS: *Carbohydrates:* 14 grams *Calories:* 148

index

conversion chart

The recipes that appear in this cookbook use the standard United States method for measuring liquid and dry or solid ingredients (teaspoons, tablespoons, and cups). The information on this chart is provided to help cooks outside the U.S. successfully use these recipes. All equivalents are approximate.

METRIC EQUIVALENTS FOR DIFFERENT TYPES OF INGREDIENTS

A standard cup measure of a dry or solid ingredient will vary in weight depending on the type of ingredient. A standard cup of liquid is the same volume for any type of liquid. Use the following chart when converting standard cup measures to grams (weight) or milliliters (volume).

Standard Cup	Fine Powder (e.g. flour)	Grain (e.g. rice)	Granular (e.g. sugar)	Liquid Solids (e.g. butter)	Liquid (e.g. milk)
1	140 g	150 g	190 g	200 g	240 ml
¾	105 g	113 g	143 g	150 g	180 ml
⅔	93 g	100 g	125 g	133 g	160 ml
½	70 g	75 g	95 g	100 g	120 ml
⅓	47 g	50 g	63 g	67 g	80 ml
¼	35 g	38 g	48 g	50 g	60 ml
⅛	18 g	19 g	24 g	25 g	30 ml

EQUIVALENTS FOR LIQUID INGREDIENTS BY VOLUME

¼ tsp	=				1 ml
½ tsp	=				2 ml
1 tsp	=				5 ml
3 tsp	=	1 tbls	=	½ fl oz =	15 ml
		2 tbls	=	⅛ cup =	1 fl oz = 30 ml
		4 tbls	=	¼ cup =	2 fl oz = 60 ml
		5⅓ tbls	=	⅓ cup =	3 fl oz = 80 ml
		8 tbls	=	½ cup =	4 fl oz = 120 ml
		10⅔ tbls	=	⅔ cup =	5 fl oz = 160 ml
		12 tbls	=	¾ cup =	6 fl oz = 180 ml
		16 tbls	=	1 cup =	8 fl oz = 240 ml
		1 pt	=	2 cups =	16 fl oz = 480 ml
		1 qt	=	4 cups =	32 fl oz = 960 ml
					33 fl oz = 1000 ml = 1l

USEFUL EQUIVALENTS FOR DRY INGREDIENTS BY WEIGHT

(To convert ounces to grams, multiply the number of ounces by 30.)

1 oz	=	$1/16$ lb	=	30 g
4 oz	=	¼ lb	=	120 g
8 oz	=	½ lb	=	240 g
12 oz	=	¾ lb	=	360 g
16 oz	=	1 lb	=	480 g

USEFUL EQUIVALENTS FOR COOKING/OVEN TEMPERATURES

	Fahrenheit	Celsius	Gas Mark
Freeze Water	32° F	0° C	
Room Temperature	68° F	20° C	
Boil Water	212° F	100° C	
Bake	325° F	160° C	3
	350° F	180° C	4
	375° F	190° C	5
	400° F	200° C	6
	425° F	220° C	7
	450° F	230° C	8
Broil			Grill